# THE SOCIAL CHARTER
## AND THE
## SINGLE EUROPEAN MARKET

# The
# SOCIAL CHARTER
## *and the*
# SINGLE EUROPEAN MARKET

*Towards a Socially Responsible
Community*

JOHN HUGHES

SPOKESMAN
for
EUROPEAN LABOUR FORUM

We thank the Trade Union Research Unit (TURU) at Ruskin College, Oxford,
for making available this text.

First published in Great Britain in 1991 by:
Spokesman
Bertrand Russell House
Gamble Street
Nottingham, England
Tel. 0602 708318

British Library Cataloguing in Publication Data

Hughes, John 1927-
    Social charter and the single European market: towards a socially
    responsible community. — (European labour forum v. 1)
    1. European Economic Community. Social Charter
    I. Title   II. Series
    323.094

ISBN 0-85124-523-4
ISBN 0-85124-524-2 pbk

Printed by the Russell Press Ltd, Nottingham
(Tel. 0602 784505)

# CONTENTS

# Foreword

In the heady days before the European Elections in 1989, the Social Charter succeeded, perhaps for the first time, in making headlines about the European Community which dissolved the prevailing boredom that was normally provoked by that entity. Indeed, it actually induced something close to enthusiasm among British trade unionists. Of course, the ground had been well prepared.

When Jacques Delors visited the Trade Union Congress as a star guest, his message brought the right news at the right time.

The long Thatcher years had eroded one after another of the gains achieved in social welfare during the postwar years. Freedom of trade union action had been ringed around again and again and again. Local democracy had been circumscribed, while a hurricane of hostile measures shattered the powers of Local Councillors to act in defence of their constituents, in one vital area after another. National democracy was contracting, in an authoritarian climate. Economic power had been very largely transferred to international institutions. The British state was now largely hostile territory. Old ideas of consensus had been displaced, and entry to God's Heavenly Kingdom would henceforth take place by competitive tender.

The President of the European Commission found avid listeners to his alternative appeal, and not only among his chosen audience.

Suddenly, a new prophet had arisen in Brussels. Was it possible that all those causes which had been lost during the Great Waste since 1979, all those social Goods, could now, after ten corrosive years, be recovered in the European Community?

Mrs Thatcher instantly understood these hopes. She was always sensitive to the danger of shared aspirations and collective action, and her political will reacted to these qualities with the force of a laser. "Socialism through the back door!" she responded. President Delors was cast in the unlikely role of Marxist subversive. He was undermining the free market, and restoring collectivism, red in tooth and claw. Britain had not liquidated gas and water socialism in all its crumbling municipalities, in order to see an outbreak of profligate and indiscriminate welfare imposed from Brussels.

Surprisingly this message of uncontrolled individualism, once welcomed by people from different social classes, now provoked antagonism from one end of Britain's social space to the other. The rat race had been reluctantly accepted in a condition in which there was "no alternative". But now this argument between Thatcher and Delors made it perfectly clear that real alternatives could exist. The Labour Party, far from being over-run by national Thatcherism, suddenly recovered. Forty-five Labour Members were returned to the European Parliament in June 1989, and almost all the other Members elected turned out to be "wet" Conservatives who were profoundly uneasy about the xenophobic policies decreed by their leader.

There can be no doubt that the Social Charter contributed, most powerfully, to this result. For the first time, co-ordinated international action in pursuit of social goals had become not only thinkable, but even practical. Millions of people might expect to benefit from such action. In a short time, British pensioners became aware of something of the vast gap which separated them from their more affluent continental neighbours. Discrimination against women was perceived to be all the worse when compared with normal European standards. Trade union and employment rights stood revealed in all their poverty, once a European yardstick had become available. It was not only possible, but necessary, to vote for an attempt to open the door on such social legislation. Nobody minded whether the door in question was at the back or the front of the European Community. The very idea that there were two doors was a death blow to the Thatcher prescription, which depended on its power to persuade all to enter the one approved portal.

Immediately after the 1989 Elections, the counter-pressures were focused. The Socialist Group became the largest political Party in Strasbourg. But no sooner had it celebrated its victory by publishing a leaflet on the Social Charter, all bedecked with roses, than the first reverses became apparent. Just as the animals in George Orwell's famous fable watched as the commandments which had been whitewashed on the barn wall were slowly altered, so European socialists began to see the Charter's crucial points amended and nibbled away. National governments, led by the British, squeezed as hard as they could. The Commission began to adjust. A promise to provide a guaranteed minimum *income* was transmuted to become a minimum *wage*. Alarm bells began to ring. As early as November 1989, there took place the first Parliamentary rebellion.

This story continues, and will no doubt burst into the public limelight again. President Delors himself has warned, at the beginning of 1991, that he finds the failure to progress the Social Charter "particularly disappointing". Unless more rapid progress can be made, it is perfectly possible that Parliamentarians will seek to block other types of legislation, in order to speed up the fulfilment of social promises.

But whatever happens in the Parliament, the key influence of the Social Charter will be exercised among that wider public which has responded to its call. Community pressure groups, women's organisations, pensioners' societies, trade unions and other lobbies have all learnt that they have much to gain from a levelling up of standards throughout Europe. Some are beginning to join their forces, and to co-ordinate their advocacy. The Socialist Group in the Parliament has agreed to convene a Pensioners' Parliament in Brussels, in order to encourage this kind of cross-frontier co-operation. Similar dialogue has already opened between groups defending the rights of handicapped people, or promoting civil freedoms.

When this kind of initiative is transformed into joint action, Europe's social programme will have begun the creation of a truly European society: a civil polity in which each may truly stand for all, and all for each, regardless of old frontiers and disreputable prejudices.

*Ken Coates*
*March 1991*

PART ONE

# EUROPEAN SOCIAL ENGINEERING: THE ISSUES

CHAPTER 1

# The Pace Accelerates:
# The UK Government Resists

"The European Council considered that in the course of the
construction of the single European market social aspects
should be given the same importance as economic aspects
and should accordingly be developed in a balanced
fashion". (Communiqué of the European Council, Madrid,
June 1989, 'Social Dimension'.)

We can hardly understate the importance for the future
political economy of Europe of the wide-ranging
developments and changes being set in motion in the course
of constructing a "single market" for the European
Community. The widening of the Community to embrace 12
member states in the recent past (and now the unification of
Germany within that total) generates more challenges from
diversity of economic and social conditions and traditions. It
is not that we are preparing for some climactic moment; in
that sense the emphasis on 1992 is perhaps unfortunate, for
innumerable "transitions" begin before that date and will
stretch out for years after it. But what Jacques Delors calls the
"architects" are working at an accelerated pace on an
enormous range of economic and social projects. And the
consequences of the projected developments will ramify in
many directions. So the coherence and balance of the
programmes matter very much.

It is only if we are mesmerized by "short-termism" that we
can imagine that what faces us is simply "gradualism" in social
or economic reform or re-organisation. We are in a period of
major *structural* changes and challenges in the European
economy and its norms. It is simplistic to think that this is
primarily a matter of "openness" and competition. It is more

evidently the removal of many forms of economic management from national governments acting unilaterally, not least currency and credit manipulation, concealed (e.g. public sector) protectionism as well as open barriers to entry, discrimination in the labour market, and other "beggar my neighbour" policies. So we will be concerned with a search for responsibility and effectiveness in economic management in the European Community within a shared sovereignty. And as to competition, in most key market sectors this will be giant-firm (oligopolistic) competition. A crucial dimension of European economic management will be the determination of the economic and social responsibilities of those large — which means transnational — enterprises; for instance, human resource concerns, protection of the environment, the safety of both work processes and products. Single countries have not had the ability to handle the terms of that development dialogue with the world's multinationals; the emerging European Community will have.

Two interlinked dimensions of social and political concern follow from this. Firstly, the process required is not one that can or should *subordinate* wider social and political concerns to the market. The handling of the new needs both of economic management and of equity that arise from the 'single market' requires a rapid evolution of new norms (more widely responsible than before) of social and political (Community and national governmental) principle and practice. It calls for new agencies, new procedures, more transparency and the extension of democratic accountability. The acceptance of qualified majority voting across a wider range of subjects is one modest expression of this. Convergence and harmonisation accompany these shared responsibilities, in the name of equity if nothing else.

Secondly, the emerging political economy of the Community carries evident, if as yet not readily quantifiable, levels of disturbance and risk for many workers and their communities. This underlines the importance of reaching out for a wider social and political consensus for the process of change. One element of the response needed is an emphasis on dialogue and participation, involving not only workers and their organisations but other "social partners" (not forgetting consumer organisations). That continuing dialogue has to encompass and move between Community-wide and enterprise level involvement, with all the key staging posts between those. But a key to social consensus is progress on the expression and guaranteeing of social rights and opportunities. The logic here is the underpinning of existing good practice in social rights, social security, and participation; in Community parlance, "no retrogression". That, in turn, directly influences the norms asserted for 'basic' or minimum social rights across the Community; felt fairness could not emerge if the gap between underpinned good practice and the definition of social rights "fundamental" to all were too great. It would, on the one hand, damage the high trust relationship with workers and their organisations that is sought for, and plant controversy in place of construction and consensus. It would, on the other, be a denial of the "level playing field" for competitive business in the single market if business in particular sectors or countries could resort to "social dumping" (an expression widely employed in the debate) through a denial to its workers of forms and levels of protection, security, individual and collective rights, training opportunities and so on that were accepted practice elsewhere.

The logic for the Community is that these emphases on social dialogue, and on the equitable extension of social rights, need to go hand in hand with large scale programmes of expenditure helping the development and re-structuring of disadvantaged regions, tackling long-term unemployment, and the needs of young people entering the labour market, and the like. All this together constitutes the "social dimension".

The European Commission has, particularly through the voice of its President, Jacques Delors, embraced and expressed this logic. Thus,

> "Measures adopted to complete the large market should not diminish the level of social protection already achieved in the Member States . . . The internal market should be designed to benefit each and every citizen of the Community. It is necessary to improve workers' living and

working conditions and to provide better protection for their health and safety at work".*

Delors argued that the concrete progress needed included —

> "The establishment of a platform of guaranteed social rights, containing general principles, such as every worker's right to be covered by a collective agreement, and more specific measures concerning, for example, the status of temporary work.
>
> "The creation of a Statute for European Companies, which would include the participation of workers or their representatives. Those concerned could opt . . . between three formulae.
>
> "The extension to all workers of the right to life-long education".

For a time it looked as if the notion of what was required for the realisation of the "social dimension" was to be dominated by the debate over the "Community Charter of Social Rights", presented by the Commission in draft form in 1989. In a way, this was understandable because its wide scope helped the strategic approach emerge clearly in a way that would not be evident from detailed and piecemeal proposals. The *cumulative* force of its 33 points was impressive; reading it one can sense that it is a building block of a more socially responsible Community and a highly effective bid for Community-wide consensus. The language of a European Council (Social Affairs) meeting in June 1989, after an initial debate on the draft, is for once eloquent:

> "Without prejudice to any amendments which might still be made, the Council noted that there was a general consensus on the fundamental rights set out in the preliminary draft Charter and that *they constituted the social identity of the Community*".** (Author's emphasis.)

That conclusion was reached by 11 of the 12 countries of the Community, and again 11 supported the Charter in its final

*Jacques Delors: "The Social Dimension", address to TUC, 1988.
**Conclusions of 12 June 1989 presented to Madrid European Council on 26-27 June 1989.

form in the European Council meeting of December 1989. The UK was alone in refusing to make a declaration of support.

The Charter itself is a declaration, not a binding commitment. But even before the final declaration of support by all Community countries except the UK, the Commission had in November 1989 set down its Action Programme to transform many of the principles in the Charter into binding Community requirements. The Action Programme included 45 proposals, 17 involving new Directives. (A Directive once adopted is binding on member states, and specifies dates by which provisions have to be incorporated into national legislation.) The Commission is introducing fairly swiftly detailed drafts, understandably in view of the time lags involved (in formal consultation on draft Directives, quite apart from subsequent delays before national legislation is put through). There could be something of a crisis of confidence if by 1992 the 'single market' is operating as an instrument of what Schumpeter called "creative destruction", but the social protection is not in place.

The Social Charter itself, then, is not receding into history. For the Commission it is the beginning of a process of detailed work (and controversy) to make it operational, not a declamatory end in itself. Here, it is helpful somewhat briefly to set down the main headings of the ground it covers. These start with the right of freedom of movement of citizens of the European Community to engage in any occupation "on the same terms as those applied to nationals of the host country", i.e. "equal treatment" in all fields. The articles on employment and remuneration refer in a substantially undefined way to a "decent" basic wage (and the Commission proposes only to follow this up with an "opinion" on guaranteeing an "equitable" wage; a weak form of intervention). There is more bite in the reference ("rules shall be laid down") to terms of employment "other than an open-ended full-time contract".

This last point is repeated in the section on "Improvement of living and working conditions". What is spelt out is the notion of combining both an improvement and an "approximation" of conditions (i.e. levelling up and moving closer to harmonisation) particularly on working time and its maximum duration, and on part-time working and short contracts.

On "Social Protection" the Charter argues both for social security benefits "proportional" to contributions for "all" workers, and for "minimum income" arrangements and social assistance to those "unable to enter the labour market", or otherwise without "adequate means of subsistence". There is a further section devoted to the right to "freedom of association and collective bargaining". The wording here is specific and significant: "everyone has the freedom to exercise this right or to renounce it without any personal or occupational damage". The right entails "freedom to negotiate and conclude collective agreements, which should be promoted". Social rights are here both individual *and* collective. Another section couched in very specific language sets out the opportunities of vocational training to be provided to "every European Community worker" on a continuing basis. The section on "equal treatment" for men and women is equally specific; "Action shall be intensified" across a wide range of relevant issues.

At first sight the Charter includes only a modest statement in the section dealing with the right to health protection and safety at work. This should not hide the particularly strong position the Commission is in so far as this subject area is concerned. The Single European Act provided under a revised Treaty of Rome provision (Article 118A) for health and safety at work to be subject to qualified majority voting to encourage improvement and harmonisation. In this field alone 10 new Directives have been adopted or will be completed by end 1990. One of these, in 1989, added the obligation of "participation" to those for "information and consultation" as a right on workplace health and safety. The Social Charter in its section on information, consultation, and participation seeks to extend and indeed — at large company level — generalise this insistence on "participation" (it is, after all, the hallmark of dialogue and high trust), especially in companies operating "in several member states".

The Social Charter ends modestly with sections on the protection of young people at work, and elderly persons in retirement. It then invites the Commission to present not only an action programme, which it has done, but also to report "at regular intervals" on the implementation of the Charter's principles. Thus a continuing pressure through action and publicity on progress (or the lack of it) can be sustained on the social front.

A later section will explore in detail the key ingredients in the strategy of the European Commission's social "action programme", and by what processes it may develop. But one aspect should be understood at this stage. In its chosen programme, the Commission is testing its ability to proceed in important areas against the evident hostility of the UK Government. Draft Directives it knows will be bitterly contested by the UK Government are being put forward for adoption by qualified majority voting. This is being grounded on specific principles in the underlying Treaty of Rome. A challenge to this would involve testing the legitimacy of the approach at the European Court of Justice. The essentially federal nature of the constitutional and political process involved is obvious from the start.

The repeated opposition of the UK Government should not lead us to underestimate the dominating force of the broad consensus on social rights and associated interventionist policies that now exists within the Community. In the next chapter the basis of this support is reviewed. But this can usefully be prefaced by some recognition of the quite new alignment in the UK itself.

The generally hostile posture of the UK Government to the main thrust of the European Commission's proposals in the single market's "social dimension" is familiar enough, but deserves some close scrutiny. Although — astonishingly — accepting the Madrid European Council's communiqué in 1989, whose central commitment to the "social dimension" is quoted at the beginning of this chapter, its real position is quite different. As it puts it in the Department of Trade and Industry's *The Single Market: The Facts* (p.86), "The Government believes that in general a 'social Europe' will *stem from* an effective single market. This will create growth, gains in employment and prosperity, and *therefore* the climate in which improvements in social and working conditions can be negotiated". This is, of course, entirely at variance with the formally agreed Madrid position that "*in the course of the construction* of the single European market social aspects should be given *the same importance* as economic aspects". (Author's emphases.)

In its internal publications the UK Government adopts a dismissive tone, reinforced, where it feels most ill at ease, by silence. The DTI publication mentioned above (Third Edition, February 1989) gets into the subject with:

> "There is much talk in the Community of the so-called 'social dimension' to the single market, but there is as yet little clear indication of what it might entail".

Yet, the Department of Employment's later publication (undated but clearly published after the Madrid European Council meeting of June 1989) entitled *The UK in Europe: People, Jobs, and Progress* — a "Fact Pack"(!) — could not bring itself even to *mention* the Commission's draft "Charter of Fundamental Social Rights" which had been dominating discussion from May 1989. This silence was the more extraordinary since the entire function of the Department of Employment publication, with 12 separate "Fact Sheets" and much besides, was to present some explanation and justification of the UK Government's views in the debate about the social dimension: "this folder is a contribution to that debate. It sets out our approach to the social dimension". The innocent reader of the Department's "Fact Pack" was not even to be offered the "fact" of the Charter's existence; not so much Hamlet without the ghost, as the ghost without Hamlet.

Apart from wanting to *postpone* a coherent social policy until some indefinite date *after* the single market has been established, a number of strands of policy response are apparent. So far from wanting to see new minimum standards established, the emphasis is on "removal of unnecessary regulation". The Government, we are told, does *not* share the view that the Community needs a wide-ranging programme of *regulation* on employment and social issues (D of E Fact Sheet 5). The assertion repeated throughout is that job creation is the priority and that "if we burden the Community's industry with new and unnecessary regulation in the name of the social dimension, we will negate the single market itself". Beyond this, there is evidently no sympathy with any concept of reflecting the long continued Community emphasis on organised labour as a crucial "social partner", and embodying this in *collective* social rights; the D of E's very first "Fact Sheet" insists that the UK's "vision" is a Community nurturing *individual* freedom and opportunity; the issue of combining that with collective rights is passed by in silence. Consequently, we find the UK Government hostile to proposals to build into compannylaw rights of employees' participation. But in practice it has also become apparent that the UK Government is hostile to new definitions of *individual* rights such as those that would protect part-time workers against discrimination as to pay and conditions; this important issue of principle is discussed in detail later.

Yet if the UK Government's response to the "social" debate has simply been *not* to change, that debate has already had the most profound effect on the British labour movement. In what must rank as the most dramatic shift in the stance of the UK trade union movement in generations, that movement has been won over particularly by the Commission's broad social programme. It is not really possible to play down this shift by arguing that it represented a search on a European scale for the "corporatism" that had been spurned in Britain. It goes further than that. The trade unions are locked into a movement towards wider European integration and harmonisation in place of the old insularities and instinctive protectionism. They may thereby be enabled to move from the old norms of "adversarial" industrial relations practice towards a more constructive and strategic "social partnership", a crucial dimension of which will be the very *participation* in enterprise (particularly large firm) development that the Government resists. In the new logic of their changed position they have to respect the dominant European principles of respect for individual worker rights as well as collective ones, of legal frameworks for the responsible exercise of trade union power, and of a voluntary basis for membership, and a withdrawal from the old rigidities of the "closed shop". The unresolved crisis of UK industrial relations practice and of labour law can be overcome by a new framework of reference (in place of the old battleground with the Common Law) built on a move towards the most progressive European practice. The Labour Party has in consequence been able to move beyond its old ambivalence (based on internal disagreement) about its commitment to a wider Europe, and in so doing to become — if it reaches political power — the agency also of a more consensual system of industrial relations and industrial democracy for the UK. This process of conversion of the principles and goals of the UK's labour movement, although it has much further to go, is of far more profound significance than the absence of any equivalent move towards a European consensus on the part of a section of the Conservative Party which currently monopolises political power.

# CHAPTER 2

# The Social Dimension: Sources of European Support

The UK Government, in its attempt to resist, delay, and dilute the carrying through of a broad Community programme of social action and harmonisation of social rights, has difficulty in identifying reliable allies elsewhere in the Community. It is for this reason that it is particularly angered when the European Commission brings forward proposed Directives grounded in principles enunciated in the underlying Treaty of Rome, and directly linked to the requirements of a future 'single market', since these open up a decision-making process involving qualified majority voting and denying the UK Government the benefit of a unilateral veto. In its publicity the UK Government is reduced to referring loosely to "Europe's employers" as supporting its resistance to social regulation. The reality is not so simple.

One factor behind the thrust for a Community-wide programme of social rights and a *levelling up* of working conditions is the concern of employers as well as governments in the high-wage, high-productivity economies of continental Europe. A dominant influence in terms of 'models' is that of Germany; dominant partly from sheer scale (in output terms the manufacturing sector is twice as large as the UK's). The "Social Market Economy" has proved a more reliable source of economic growth, low inflation, formidable competitive power in foreign trade, long-run profits growth, high wages and reduced working time than other models. There were particular historical reasons why German employers in the post-war period had to accept a socially responsible role. Thus, worker participation in the large enterprises of key sectors (co-determination) was seen as a significant element of democracy and social accountability urgently needed in the political vacuum left after the defeat of nazi rule.*

But certainly the *cumulative* outcome of co-determination, constitutional labour rights and responsibilities, massive employer-supported investment in training, powerful industrial unions, and equivalent employer organisations engaged in both industry-wide bargaining and economy-wide dialogue about national economic development needs, is that all this has been both commercially and socially effective. Such a strategy requires to be highly productive because it carries with it high indirect labour costs, including elaborate social insurance. In a common market moving towards a wider removal of barriers, high wage employers of this kind would not want to see unfair competition from nations that did not share such social commitments.

As we argued in Chapter 1, for social peace in the high wage, high social responsibility economies there had to be a commitment *not* to undermine the standards and rights already achieved. Business interest therefore lies in levelling-up elsewhere in the Community towards the social norms of the dominant model. If, as the European Commission argues, the wide variation in wage levels in member states is broadly matched by differences in productivity, so that unit pay costs are roughly similar, there is all the more reason to attack the 'distortion' of competition involved, if 'social dumping', the avoidance of social responsibilities in the labour market, were to be tolerated.

These factors have been linked with the moral — and political — force of organisations with shared value systems that reach beyond business interests or particular frontiers. Catholicism with its challenge to untramelled capitalism and its respect for labour (while emphasising its responsibilities) has been an important influence. Consequently, in many respects that bear directly upon the dimension of social policies, Christian Democratic parties have a good deal in

*In the immediate post-war years the British Control Commission in Western Germany played an important part in installing co-determination in heavy industry. It seems ironic that the barely re-formed German trade union movement was (rightly) trusted with this far-reaching task while at the same time in the UK the trade unions were being restricted in their participation role in the management of newly nationalised industries to a limited and formal consultation process.

common across national frontiers and can be contrasted with the insular peculiarities of the Conservative Party in the UK. Catholicism has also played a role in trade union organisation in countries where Communist parties and Communist influenced trade union organisations have been strong. Jacques Delors embodies this fusion of trade union solidarity and collectivism with Catholic social values. But we should recognise also the great importance of a European secular tradition of social democratic parties and of trade unions sympathetic to social democracy. With the moral collapse of intransigent Communist modes of organisation and their assumptions of social conflict, the popular appeal and organisational force of the social democratic tradition is enhanced. What we now see in the European Parliament, for instance, is a broad alliance of Christian Democratic and Social Democratic members of parliament forming an effective majority and capable of pressing for a strong development of the European Commission's social policies. (We also see isolation of the small UK Conservative group of MEPs in the European Parliament.)

In consequence, even at this immature stage of the development of the federal elements of the Community, and even while its own direct democratic elements are so hemmed in, the European Community does have the capacity to press on with a major social programme, centred on social responsibility and rights in the European labour market.

PART TWO

# COMMUNITY PROCESSES
# AND THE
# SOCIAL ACTION PROGRAMME

CHAPTER 3

# The Process and its Problems

As one might expect, developing legislation that will be applied across the Community is a lengthy and complex process. Much of the decision-making process derives from the inter-action of the Commission and the Council. The *Commission* itself is made up of 17 members appointed by the member governments (two each from France, Germany, Italy, Spain, and the UK, one each from the other member states) but acting in the interests of the whole Community. The Commission has initiative in proposing Community policy and legislation, as well as acting as guardian of the EC rules, able to initiate action against non-compliance by any member state. The *Council* is shorthand for Ministers from all the member states; functionally it operates through working groups of officials, Councils of Ministers relevant to particular subjects, and now, twice a year, a European Council of heads of state/government discussing broad policy. It may 'adopt' legislation proposed by the Commission, or block proposals. Where the Treaties provide for decision-making by unanimous vote, a single country can exercise a veto. But the Single European Act (1987) extended the scope of 'qualified majority' voting in the Council to most single market proposals. 'Qualified majority' voting relates voting to the relative population size of member states. To adopt a proposal 54 positive votes out of a total of 76 are required. (This means a proposal could go through against the opposition of even two of the largest members if all other states voted in favour.)

So one of the important issues in seeking to implement the social dimension of the single market is whether the Commission can bring a proposal forward resting on the legal base of articles in the underlying EC Treaty that would permit qualified majority voting. Thus, at the time of the Single European Act, the Treaty was amended by Article 118A providing for qualified majority voting on proposals to encourage improvements in the working environment, on health and safety of workers, and harmonisation of conditions in these areas. But quite how wide *is* the scope of "the working environment"? In 1990 one of the draft Directives put forward by the Commission on Part-Time Workers (to be examined in more detail subsequently) is resting on the Treaty article prohibiting practices that distort competition between member states, so as to make it subject to qualified majority voting.

When the Commission brings forward proposals on economic and social matters it has to send them to the Economic and Social Committee of the Community, which has rights of a consultative nature. The ESC is made up of representatives of employers, trade unions, and other interests including consumers, small firms and professions. The proposals also go to the European Parliament (the only directly elected body) whose formal opinion has to be received before the Council can adopt a Commission proposal. More significantly, if the Council adopts proposals by a qualified majority, their "common position" is referred to the European Parliament for a second reading. If Parliament rejects the common position by an absolute majority, Council can then only act by adopting a proposal on the subject by unanimity. If the European Parliament amends the Council's common position (again, by an absolute majority), the Commission has to review the amendments and *may* revise its proposals before putting them again before the Council for adoption by qualified majority.*

These procedures, then, are protracted ones, the more so when qualified majority voting is used, even if there is a high degree of consensus on the issue being tackled. But this is not the only time-lag involved; it depends on the type of Community legislation involved. *Regulations* have general application and apply directly in all member states without

---

*It is worth noting that the Council can only successfully amend a Commission proposal (and this applies to European Parliament amendments that the Commission doesn't approve) by unanimity.

any further process of confirmation by national parliaments. They are suitable where an identical law is required across the Community; for instance, the statute for a European Company — if adopted — would be a Regulation. But in the field of social policy it is much more likely that the Commission would be seeking to issue *Directives*. Directives are more suitable as an instrument where the method of implementation may vary at the level of member states (either because the Commission and Council wish a range of choices to be available, or because the measure has to be related to existing laws or orders in the subject area in a particular country). A *Directive* becomes binding on member states so far as the results that are to be achieved within a stated period — thus building in another time-lag.

But what if a member state does not develop suitable legislation in the subject area of a Directive by the due date? The Commission has the task of monitoring compliance with obligations under the Treaty and can therefore refer the issue to the *European Court of Justice*. In what is really a federal system some form of supreme court is needed to adjudicate on the interpretation of Community law, and this is the European Court's function. It is quite possible, at the moment, that the UK Government might seek to test at the European Court whether the Commission was right in resting proposed Directives in the social field on articles in the Treaty that enabled qualified majority voting, to be used.

For all these reasons, unless the Commission can bring forward its Directives and other proposals on social policy subjects with urgency and carry them through Council with qualified majority voting, there is a clear risk that the threshold date for the single market will arrive without the key measures of social rights and protection in place. The credibility of the "balanced fashion" in which the social and the economic aspects of constructing the single market were to be put in place is at stake.

# CHAPTER 4

# Key Elements in the Social Action Programme

In formulating its "Action Programme" the Commission has had to reflect both on strategy and on tactics. The 11 to 1 vote for the Social Charter does offer some sources of strength as well as the need to avoid the expenditure of effort on proposals that would become a victim of a UK veto. The Commission is committed to presenting "at regular intervals" reports on the implementation of the principles of the Charter, so that it can publicise both progress and lack of it. It can encourage piecemeal advances on a broad range of subjects, where member governments and relevant interest groups are sympathetic, and to some extent shape such developments by issuing formal "Opinions" and "Recommendations". These latter do not have any binding force, but may help encourage particular responses; the Commission places emphasis on using such Recommendations to achieve "convergence", i.e. to move towards harmonisation of policy and practice. This approach is to be adopted, for the time being, on the question of the minimum wage; one can imagine that at some later stage such an issue might become ripe for tackling through a Directive.

We should remember also that a number of important pieces of social legislation are already in place. Thus the equal pay directive was followed up by a 1986 Directive on equal treatment in occupational social security schemes, due for implementation in 1993. In health and safety the key "Framework Directive", setting out the responsibilities of employers and workers and imposing organisational requirements (including worker consultation and participation), is already in place. In the words of the TUC, "The EC is now firmly established as the major force in the development of new health and safety legislation". The Commission itself emphasises as a complementary part of its strategy for workers' interests its success in gaining Council agreement in 1989 for massive expenditure on structural funds to "increase the solidarity of the Community". Delors estimated that between 1989 and 1992 some £40 billion will be devoted to development of the backward regions of the Community, restructuring regions in economic decline, acting against long-term unemployment, and providing jobs for young people. In its documentation of the social action programme the Commission stresses the importance it gives to its monitoring and assessment of these programmes.

Conscious of the constraints created by the lengthy time-lags between proposals and their adoption, the Commission has put "the most urgent priorities" of the social action programme in its 1990 work programme. These include a Directive on the re-organisation of working time, in particular setting out restrictions on night-work and shift work, and minimum rest periods. This revives an attempt at a Directive on these lines in 1985 which foundered on disagreement in the Council. These proposed minima would certainly have some effective bite in the UK; for instance, the proposed restriction of nightwork to eight hours in any 24 would challenge such things as the 11 hour nightshifts worked by nurses in the NHS. The draft Directive also sets out to limit systematic overtime, a major weakness in UK practice (more so than on the Continent) which we have so far been unable to control through collective bargaining.

Other draft Directives also return to an earlier unsuccessful bid by the Commission (this time in 1982). This proposal relates to part-time workers and seeks in essence to prevent widespread discrimination against them by pursuing the principle of "pro-rata" treatment, as compared to full-time workers, on both wages and conditions of work, including training. The new draft Directives also embrace other "atypical" work contracts (which in 1982 had been the subject of a separate Directive) relating to temporary work and fixed-term contracts. The next chapter is devoted to an examination in detail of these draft Directives and the debate they have already stirred up, so that the reader can grasp in more depth the significant issues that are now raised by their heading the "action programme".

The Commission is also re-opening discussion suspended by the Council in 1986 on a draft Directive for the procedures for information, consultation and participation of workers in "European-scale undertakings". This goes alongside a draft Directive on workers' participation which the Commission has firmly attached to the draft Regulation for a European Company Statute. The participation Directive allows a choice of three modes of participation: election of worker representatives to a supervisory board; election of worker representatives to a separate body (in this and the previous 'option' with sweeping rights to demand information and prior consultation on major development matters); or collectively agreed systems decided upon by the workforce and the management at company level. This European Company Statute and its associated Directive is proceeding on a basis that allows for qualified majority voting. In the "action programme" the Commission is seeking to "generalise" participatory principles where undertakings are "European-scale" (whether they adopt the European Company Statute form or not).

In tackling what are best thought of as companies operating as multinational enterprises within the Community, the Commission's argument is clear-cut and relevant to the single market:

> "As information and consultation procedures do not apply beyond national boundaries, employees affected by decisions taken elsewhere by the main undertaking . . . could be unequally treated. The situation is bound to have a direct effect on the operation of the internal market and on the multiplication of mergers, take-overs and concentration of enterprises resulting therefrom. It would therefore be desirable to improve the information and consultation of the workers of these companies . . ."*

The approach is designed to weaken the position of any national government resisting such proposals. Apart from

*Commission Communication on its Action Programme, COM (89)568, p.32.

fitting in with notions of social equity and harmonisation, it moves against distortion of competition in the internal market. It also fits neatly into the Community notion rather strangely known as "subsidiarity". The notion essentially is that the Community acts when the set objective can be reached more *effectively* at its level than at that of the Member States. (There is, of course, a UK Government deviant doctrine which alleges that the principle of "subsidiarity" means that "you should do at Community level only what cannot be done at national level".*) The Commission is therefore picking its ground quite carefully.

The Commission's intention is to move from a fresh discussion at Council level of the earlier "Vredeling" proposal for a Directive to "consultation with the social partners" leading to the drafting of a new "Community instrument" containing the following principles:

"(a) Establishment of equivalent systems of worker representation in all European-scale enterprises.
(b) General and periodic information should be provided regarding the development of the enterprise as it affects the employment and interests of workers.
(c) Information must be provided and consultations should take place before taking any decisions liable to have serious consequences for the interests of employees, in particular, closures, transfers, curtailment of activities, substantial changes with regard to organisation, working practices, production methods, long-term co-operation with other undertakings, etc.
(d) The dominant associated undertakings shall provide the information necessary for the employer to inform the employees' representatives".**

As a Community information memo puts it, the Commission is arguing the necessity of putting "such procedures on a general footing so as to ensure that unavoidable restructuring is carried out under socially acceptable conditions".

All these major initiatives are linked to a programme of measures of more limited individual scope. For instance, a revised Directive on Collective Redundancy, to cover cases

*Department of Employment: *UK in Europe*. Fact Sheet No.9.
**Commission, op.cit.,p.33.

where the redundancy decision is taken by an undertaking in another country; revised Directives and Regulations on freedom of movement and rights to remain after employment, including the extension of the application of social security schemes to all insured persons; the introduction of a "social clause" in connection with the opening up of public works contracts; a clutch of further industry-specific Directives on health and safety; continuing pressure on the Council to deal with draft Directives already submitted on aspects of equal treatment such as parental leave, retirement age, burden of proof; a Directive on the protection of young people taking up employment; a proposed Directive to improve the safety and mobility of disabled people, particularly in the working environment; and one on the protection of pregnant women at work.

Taking it all in all, the Commission is clearly not going to leave the Social Charter as a mere element in gesture politics. Behind the scatter of measures one can see some clear principles of social protection and harmonisation. Beyond that, the Commission understandably assume that multi-national businesses will of necessity want to be strongly established in the single market. The Commission's clear intention is that to so establish themselves multinationals will have to accept rules of social responsibility, not least in terms of their workforces. European social policy is coming in from the margins, and may even occupy centre-stage.

# CHAPTER 5

# Employment and Cumulative Disadvantage

*The European Commission's Proposals on Part-Time and Temporary Workers and the Issues Involved*

To start with there is an evident problem of terminology. Our vocabulary lacks an appropriate term to encompass the wide range of workers who are working part-time, on casualised or short fixed-term contracts (broadly 'temporary' workers), or as the Commission is driven to put it "contracts and employment relationships other than full-time open-ended contracts". Indeed, if we take the Commission's approach just quoted we should be including — as they are not — such things as labour-only sub-contracting.

The Commission uses the term "atypical" contracts. That seems quite inappropriate. Such contract relationships as "casualisation" have played a major role in the history of capitalism, so have fixed-term contracts. Indeed, in the capitalist labour market one could well say that there has been nothing more permanent than the temporary. Nor can one refer to part-time working as "atypical" when in a country like Britain, where female participation in the labour force is particularly high by European standards, some 42 per cent of the total recorded number of female employees in employment are part-time (1988 data).

In the 1980s the discussion of the phenomenon took on renewed life because it was, correctly, perceived as an expanding part of the labour force, certainly in Britain. A distinction was developed between "core" labour force and "peripheral" groups. The choice of words is understandable if we see the issue as one of the predominant attitude of the *employer*, reluctant to extend rights, training, and minimisation of the worker's employment and income risk beyond a chosen "core". The language at least identifies the very *attitudes* and practices of discrimination (in Eurospeak, "social dumping") that constitute the policy problem. But we should doubly hesitate before adopting the term "peripheral"; these workers are *not* in terms of the realities of the composition of the labour market "peripheral". The argument is the same as that directed against the labelling of many millions of workers as "atypical", but goes further. It is *not,* for instance, "peripheral" to the effective organisation of retail trade meeting consumer needs by extended opening hours throughout the week to employ (if they can attract them) part-time workers: it is virtually essential in commercial terms. Nor, given the present social context of the family and child-rearing responsibilities, is it socially "peripheral" that the great bulk of these part-timers are women. But beyond the unsuitability of the word peripheral as recording economic function or social reality is the danger that it may capture the wrong *moral* assumption. "Peripheral" may build into the minds of the users the assumption that labour markets' social rights are not for these workers.

On the contrary, the crucial *moral* issue is that if "core" workers' rights (by whatever route secured, through law *and* collective bargaining) are maintained and *strengthened,* but *these* workers' rights are ignored or marginalised ("peripheral"), then in the very name of "social rights" *discrimination* in the labour market is intensified. For this reason the matters — and the ordinary people — involved in the proposed Directive are the moral touchstone of the Community's "social dimension". The Commission, Governments, the European Parliament, the social partners, have to decide:

—are we talking about the social rights of *some* or of *all?*
—are we talking about the social rights of the stronger and  better organised or of the weaker and more disadvantaged  *also?*

Nor, to pursue the problem of vocabulary further, can we pursue the topic by using the word 'flexibility'. That word is both bland (because the *costs* of flexibility can be transferred to the part-time or temporary worker, while the *benefits* accrue to the employers) and blurred (since for greater labour efficiency we may need more functional flexibility through the entire labour force). The old vocabulary through which these issues were discussed distinguished between the "primary" and the "secondary" labour market, and that language is perhaps more neutral and less pejorative than others.

## What the Commission has to say

In introducing its intention to bring forward a draft Directive "on contracts and employment relationships other than full-time open-ended contracts" the Commission had this to say:

> "This proposal is of great importance. More precisely, even if what are termed 'atypical' forms of employment are contested in some quarters, they nonetheless constitute an important component in the organisation of the labour market. For example, part-time working in all its forms, casual work and fixed-term working have grown considerably in recent years, often in a quite anarchical manner. Unless safeguards are introduced, there is a danger of seeing the development of terms of employment such as to cause problems of social dumping, or even the distortion of competition, at Community level".

This statement seems a very model of understatement, at least in terms of the situation in the UK, which is analysed below. If there is a "danger" it is one that has been operational on a growing scale for many years, and intensified by the practice of the 1980s.

The proposals of the Commission's draft Directives dealing with part-time and temporary workers aim to provide for such workers treatment equal to that accorded to "typical" full-time employees. Since discrimination against such workers takes many forms, the Directives have to embrace employment and working conditions, access to training, and social security and other measures of social protection.

The Commission has come forward with three Directives in this subject area, each based on different articles of the Treaty of Rome, and each tackling a different segment of the range of issues involved. For two of these Directives the Commission is grounding its proposals on Articles in the Treaty that would permit qualified majority voting on the part of the European Council. However, the first of these Directives (linked to Article 100), which contains key provisions relating to equal treatment for part-time and other "atypical" workers does appear to be exposed to a unanimous voting requirement, i.e. the threat of UK government veto.*

This first draft Directive emphasises the principle of the harmonisation of laws relating to working conditions and is concerned to ensure that employers provide equal treatment: part-time and temporary workers "shall be entitled to enjoy the same treatment as workers employed full time for an indefinite period". The second Directive emphasises harmonisation of laws on employment relationships so as to eliminate "distortions of competition" in the context of the single market (Article 100a). It is directed to member states and the statutory framework affecting the indirect labour costs of part-time and temporary workers as compared with typical full-time workers. It requires "social protection" — and this applies to statutory and occupational social security provision — to be "underpinned by the same groundwork and the same criteria". Member states "shall ensure that part-time workers are afforded the same entitlements to annual holidays, dismissal allowances and seniority allowances as full-time employees, in proportion to the total hours worked".** The third draft Directive extends health and safety protection for temporary workers (Article 118a).

Such a challenge to current practices of both employers and member states that discriminate against part-time workers would be undermined if there were too high a "threshold" of weekly working hours below which protection would not apply. Previous UK experience has been that a high threshold positively invites and encourages the manipulation of part-time workers' hours and pay so as to exclude them from protection (and its costs to employers). The Commission's draft Directives have gone for a comparatively low "threshold" by excluding only those part-time workers whose average weekly hours are less than eight. Such a provision would

*European Parliament News (UK edition), 22-26 October 1990, reports the Parliament sending this Directive back to committee as MEPs wanted it changed to allow a qualified majority decision by Council rather than unanimity.
**Text of draft Council Directive as quoted in the Department of Employment's "Consultative Document", August 1990.

encompass the great majority of part-time workers and powerfully challenge the patterns of statutory discrimination hitherto applied in the UK — as the next section of this chapter demonstrates.

The draft Directives would also prevent companies employing workers with "temporary" status through a series of short but renewed contracts; the draft proposes setting a limit of 36 months to such repeated denial of permanent status. Very significantly, too, both part-time and temporary workers are intended under the Commission's proposals to "enjoy access to vocational training initiated by the undertaking under conditions comparable to those enjoyed by workers employed full time for an indefinite duration, account being taken of the duration of work and the nature of the tasks to be carried out."

Thus, over the wide range of working conditions and social security provision it is intended that the "typical" or "core" workers' norms and opportunities should apply to part-time and temporary workers. Open discrimination directed at the present most vulnerable under-class of employees would be challenged on many fronts.

**The situation in Britain**

It is useful to start with overall data on employees in employment, and the changing balance between full and part-time work. The following table makes a 10 year comparison starting with the very reliable data from the 1978 Census of Employment. A 10 year comparison gives an opportunity for longer term trends to become evident; it is also helpful that both 1978 and 1988 represent similar points in the business cycle (so that comparisons are not distorted by comparing different phases in successive cycles of employment).

Over the decade we find a fall of 1¼ million in full-time employees in employment, concentrated on male full-timers whose employment fell by 1.6 million (a fall of 13 per cent). This displacement of male employees is partly reflected in higher unemployment, partly in earlier retirement, and partly associated with a considerable switch to 'self-employment'. Over the period, part-time employment rose by ¾ million (up

**Table 1:**
**Great Britain: Employees in Employment**
**(in thousands)**

|  | *June 1978* | *June 1988* | *Change, '78/'88* |
|---|---|---|---|
| MALES |  |  |  |
| Full-time | 12,396 | 10,787 | − 1,609 |
| Part-time | 704 | 919 | + 215 |
| FEMALES |  |  |  |
| Full-time | 5,486 | 5,829 | + 343 |
| Part-time | 3,688 | 4,218 | + 530 |
| ALL EMPLOYEES |  |  |  |
| Full-time | 17,882 | 16,616 | − 1,266 |
| Part-time | 4,392 | 5,137 | + 745 |

**Sources:** Census of Employment, June 1978; revised Government estimates for June 1988, *Employment Gazette*, April 1990.

17 per cent); the proportional increase was greater for part-time males than for female employees. As the table shows, by the late 1980s nearly a quarter of total employees in employment were part-time.

Given the large scale of part-time work in Britain, it must follow that *if* such workers are subject to effective discrimination in pay and conditions, and to employer avoidance of social obligations, as compared to full-time workers the aggregate effect is large enough to distort competition significantly both in the domestic market (including displacement of full-time workers*) and in overseas trade. (In 1988 just under half the UK's total trade in goods and services was with the rest of the Community.) But it is important to bear in mind also that *over 80 per cent* of part-time employees in the case of Britain are women workers, and that they constitute some 42 per cent of all women employees at work. Consequently, consistent evidence of discrimination against part-timers indicates an enormous breach in the declared principle of equal pay for work of equal value for men and women. The European Community can hardly uphold the "equal treatment" principle

*The competitive process in any capitalist economy includes the operation of the labour market; comparative costs may create widespread substitution effects, and this must be affected by avoidance of social costs in relation to part-time employment.

for the nearly six million full-time female employees in Britain but *not* for the nearly 4½ million part-timers. Still less could it seriously argue that the principle is not being breached because there are 900,000 male part-timers who may *also* be discriminated against. The treatment of part-timers is the most important test in practice of the "equal treatment" principle.

The systematic discrimination against both part-time and temporary workers in the British labour market is not, in fact, in doubt. It is substantially summed up in the following quotation from the 1986 report, *Changing Working Patterns*, prepared for the National Economic Development Office in association with the Department of Employment. It used extensive survey work by the Institute of Manpower Studies, though mentioning and drawing upon other studies. To bring out more sharply the issues directly involved here, we have emphasized parts of the text:

"The most widespread finding was of *substantially worse conditions* (non-pay benefits) of employment for most peripheral workers than those enjoyed by core workers. The principal difference here related to the provision of occupational pensions; peripheral workers in the firms interviewed were generally excluded from membership of such schemes, whether contributory or non-contributory . . .

"It was clear from our discussions that one result of the growing segmentation of the internal labour market has been to distinguish one group of workers, for whom respondents were increasingly ready to bear the dynamic costs of adjustment to change (the core group) from another, for whom they were less willing to do this. *These costs include training and retraining,* relocation, pay maintenance, pensions, career development costs, etc. In general, our respondents regarded these costs as a necessary expenditure to secure what functional flexibility they sought. But where it was not sought, i.e. from peripheral workers, there was evidence *not only of a reluctance to meet them, but of a readiness to avoid them if possible — by transferring them to the workers themselves, to the state or to other employers* . . . Beyond restricted familiarisation and on-the-job training, respondents did not generally see the need to engage in training and retraining for peripheral workers". (*Op.cit.*, p.77 and p.82.)

So far as part-timers specifically were concerned, the industry surveys in the NEDO report are revealing. Thus, in retailing the widespread use of part-timers was not only "the need to match manning levels during the day and during the week to fluctuations in customer demand" but in addition

"we found the further incentive of lower non-pay hourly costs cited by *all* our retailing respondents (saving on National Insurance contributions and pension schemes mainly) and *lower pay rates in a quarter of them* . . . Organisation of shift systems and jobs was carried out with an eye towards further cost savings — principally through *the construction of shift systems which would keep earnings below NI '(National Insurance)' threshold levels* . . . but also through *limiting job content in such a way as to permit and justify an hourly rate pay differential* between full- and part-timers. *Some companies were aware . . . of the danger of indirect sex discrimination if part-timers received a lower rate*". (*Op.cit.*, pp.25-26.)

In particular case studies cited it was also clear that lower non-pay costs associated with part-timers included savings on sick and holiday pay.

The legislation governing such subjects as National Insurance and qualifications for various employment rights has in the UK strongly reinforced the general tendency for part-time workers to be discriminated against in terms of pay and conditions by employers. The general point has previously been made that if such legislation sets different standards depending on the length of average weekly working time, or weekly pay, this invites manipulation of patterns of working time by employers as a device to avoid also the kind of obligations that arise from the continued employment of full-time workers. Part-time workers and temporary workers suffer *directly* as a result; full-time workers may suffer by being displaced from jobs by the "rigged" competition in the labour market arising from being able to avoid social costs, etc. in the case of "peripheral" workers.

The existing National Insurance system in the UK has this effect of inviting discriminatory manipulations of employment as a result of a "threshold" that is not set in terms of weekly hours but as a money sum (normally raised each year in line with inflation). Below the given sum (in 1990-91, £46 weekly earnings) neither employees nor employers pay contributions. Above that sum, they do. If the employer manipulates the extent of part-timers' weekly hours and pay to stay under that threshold this is a straightforward cost saving; a readily available tax avoidance. The employee is not similarly advantaged by exclusion; *inside* the National Insurance system they are building up entitlement to state benefits (including pension benefits) as of right. The exclusion from National Insurance of part-timers is on a massive scale (and is likely to involve particularly the most vulnerable, disadvantaged, and — in hourly terms — low paid). The UK Government itself estimates that the European Commission's proposed Directive relating to part-time workers, which would have the effect of drawing into National Insurance all those working eight or more hours weekly:-

— would thereby bring *one and three-quarter million additional part-time workers* into National Insurance contributions and benefit entitlements;

— these additional workers would contribute some £130 million (at 1990 rates) and *their employers would have to pay a "similar figure"*.

These employers are, therefore, currently avoiding some £130 million a year of social security obligations. By 1991-2 the figure would rise to nearer £150 millions. All this adds up to quite a measurable "distortion of competition".

As a further example, the present provision in the UK regarding the qualifying period for certain employment rights is clearly biased against part-time workers. For those working 16 hours or more per week the qualifying period for statutory redundancy payments and protection against unfair dismissal is 2 years (it has been lengthened since the period of the NEDO study that we have been discussing). This, of course, encourages manipulation by employing full-time workers on "temporary" contracts of shorter duration. But for part-timers working eight hours per week but less than 16 hours the qualifying period is *5 years!*\* Clearly, statutory discrimination of this kind represents an unholy alliance of manipulation against the part-time worker on the part of the state and of the employer enlarging the area of unequal treatment.

Similar patterns of discrimination were found by the NEDO survey in relation to temporary workers. The UK Government estimates that some five per cent of employees are temporary workers. The figure may be as low as that because of widespread use of sub-contracting with extensive use of 'self-employed' (it is significant that virtually all the increase in 'self-employment' in the Community has occurred in the UK). The NEDO study indicates that one strategy used by companies to increase labour market flexibility is that known as 'distancing', i.e. shifting away from pay contracts to sub-contracting, franchising, etc. to "export to others the risk and uncertainty involved". About 70 per cent of respondent firms in the survey work for the NEDO study had sought to increase 'distancing' since 1980. So the UK increase in self-employment is in part a phenomenon linked to the same concerns that have also led to increased use of temporaries since 1980; the NEDO survey team could not in fact make a clear distinction between permanent and temporary employment, and were driven to use a definition (see p.17 of *Changing Working Patterns*) of employment as recognised by firm and worker to be for a limited period "whether or not the worker is actually employed by that firm, by an employment agency or is self-employed". The estimated five per cent of the *employee* labour force who are temporary workers in the UK is, it would seem, only the part of the iceberg showing above the surface, with self-employed playing an equivalent role not counted as employees at all.

The point has already been made that temporary work contracts mean that "lack of employment continuity and security" have been transferred as a risk from the shoulders of the firm to those of the peripheral workers. In this sense a substantial proportion of UK firms seem to be 'risk averse'.

\*The data and quotations are taken from the Department of Employment's "Consultative Document" on the proposed Directives, see paragraphs A7 and A11.

But there was also, again, the manipulation of the "threshold" laid down by protective legislation. To quote the official NEDO study again:

"Firms were clearly able to arrange their affairs in such a way as largely to minimise such constraints" (i.e. protective legislation). "For example, temporary contracts were *almost always* drawn up to limit their duration to under 12 months which, for most of the period we were considering, was the minimum length of service for inclusion under the Employment Protection Act and also appeared to be the trigger for many collectively bargained rights at work". (*Op.cit.,* p.82.)

To turn from conditions to pay, we can illustrate some — but not all — of the situation of part-timers from the official annual New Earnings Survey (NES). One of the limitations of that Survey (which otherwise has many excellent strengths) is the nature of its coverage. It is based on a one per cent random sample of employees subject to income tax. The Survey Report estimates that as a result one-quarter of part-time employees are not covered; one suspects that these would include many of the most disadvantaged (since part-time pay and hours are manipulated to stay below the tax threshold as well as the National Insurance one). In terms of reliability, the Survey avoids publishing detailed analyses of male part-time earnings and concentrates on females where the much larger number of returns offers low standard errors.

In summary, the pay data can tell us the following:

(i) Female part-time hourly earnings are in general significantly lower than those of full-timers. For *manual* occupations the April 1989 NES (used in what follows, as the latest available data) shows average hourly earnings of 294p for part-time females paid adult rates, compared with 333p for full-timers (13 per cent higher). The full-time figure is one excluding overtime pay and hours to ensure strict comparability with the part-time data. The *non-manual* data, not surprisingly in view of the range of skills and career progression involved, show a much wider gap; an average of 408p for adult female part-timers hourly earnings compared with 520p for full-timers.

(ii) Industrial data for female manual workers reveals considerable *variation* in the gap between part-timers' hourly earnings and those of full-timers. For instance in food manufacturing, where unionisation and collective bargaining have over the years secured extensive application of pro rata pay, there is only a three per cent difference (319p compared with 328p). This might seem to indicate an optimum position with negligible pay discrimination. By contrast, in the important (and export orientated) "metal goods, engineering, and vehicle industries" the gap is much wider at 16 per cent (only 302p average hourly pay for part-time adult females compared to 350p for full-timers). This suggests some extent of pay discrimination against part-timers. (This is a sector where a number of equal value claims have had to be pursued in recent years, and where full-time adult male manual hourly earnings, *excluding* overtime, stand 40 per cent higher than full-time manual women's earnings — and over 60 per cent higher than part-time women's hourly earnings.)

(iii) The denial of training and career opportunities to part-time workers shows up clearly in the data relating earnings to age group. For full-timers the pattern revealed by the NES data is one of earnings rising with age for a number of years before falling moderately in later working life.

For full-time men the earnings peak is proportionately considerably higher than for full-time women and is reached later (in the 40-49 years age group). Non-manual workers as a group enjoy considerably more earnings progression than do manual workers. These patterns indicate differences in training, education and skill endowment, and career opportunities. But the earnings progression of women non-manual part-timers is far more limited than that of full-timers, and for women *manual* part-timers it is totally non-existent. Of course, individuals move between full- and part-time work, but *within* part-time work itself opportunities of pay progression are largely denied.

It is clear from the table that manual women have the least opportunities for earnings growth in adult working life. But the part-time manual women fare worst of all, with earnings slightly lower in subsequent age groups than those for age 21-24. For age groups from 25 to 49, full-time manual women

**Table 2**
**Hourly Earnings by Age Group: Part- and Full-Time Employees**
**(Gt. Britain: April 1989)**
**(In pence per hour)**

| Age Group | MANUAL Women ... Part-time | Women ... Full-time | Men Full-time | NON-MANUAL Women ... Part-time | Women ... Full-time | Men Full-time |
|---|---|---|---|---|---|---|
| 21-24 | 305.3 | 327.9 | 428.1 | 354.7 | 441.1 | 538.4 |
| 25-29 | 300.5 | 356.6 | 470.3 | 416.7 | 549.6 | 706.2 |
| 30-39 | 296.0 | 352.7 | 506.4 | 428.6 | 599.6 | 879.7 |
| 40-49 | 294.3 | 347.4 | 512.2 | 410.8 | 559.8 | 961.1 |
| 50-59 | 296.5 | 342.9 | 487.3 | 397.1 | 549.9 | 892.8 |

**Source:** NES, 1989, Parts E and F.

workers secure hourly earnings *nearly 20 per cent higher* than their part-time equivalents in the same age group. *Their* full-time pay in these age groups is nevertheless very markedly less than that of manual men; in the age range 30-49 manual men's average hourly earnings are well *over 40 per cent higher* than those of full-time manual women, and *over 70 per cent higher* than those of part-time manual women. We are here looking at the lineaments of cumulative disadvantage.

From the NES sample numbers it is clear that the great bulk of part-time women workers are in the age ranges from 30 to 59, with somewhat larger numbers in the 40-49 age group than in those on either side. But over that 30 year age range there is no sign of earnings progression.

The category of non-manual women employees is more difficult to analyse since it includes a very diverse mixture of sectors and occupations, ranging from highly skilled professional groups (such as teachers and professional medical personnel) to large sectors such as food retailing, with a high proportion of less skilled workers such as sales staff. (In food retailing average part-time non-manual women's earnings are only 275p, a very low figure below the norms of manual pay.) The age-group figures show again the inferior earnings position of part-timers. Given that the great majority of them are in age groups ranging from 30 to 59, it is significant that part-time female earnings figures average less in all those age ranges for non-manuals than those for hourly full-time women's earnings at age 21-24. Over those age ranges from 30 to 59, the part-time women's average hourly earnings are consistently less than three-quarters those of full-time non-manual women in the same age-group (and less than half those of full-time non-manual men).

This material clearly suggests that we are looking at a combination of the major earnings disadvantages affecting women in their working lives *and* the discriminatory treatment meted out to part-time workers which was analysed earlier. Access to training and opportunities for career progression in work must be part of what is required to change the situation.

(iv) Finally, on the pay of part-time workers in Britain, it is possible to compare what proportion fell below a given level of hourly earnings as contrasted with full-time workers. The 1989 NES provides us with the following information for employees paid adult rates:

**Proportion of Employees earning less than 280p an hour**

| | |
|---|---|
| Full-Time Men | 3.8% |
| Full-Time Women | 13.0% |
| Part-Time Women | 38.7% |

So, the proportion of part-time women employees below this benchmark of low pay (280p an hour) at 38.7 per cent was *three times* greater than the proportion of full-time women employees, and *ten times* greater than the proportion of full-time men. Even if we do not know how much of this difference can be explained by discrimination in pay directed at part-time workers, we can at least argue that those workers should not have their problems of low pay intensified by the toleration of discriminatory practices in pay and conditions.

## UK critics of the Commission's proposals

The Secretary of State for Employment is quoted (*Financial Times*, 14 June 1990) on receipt of the Commission's proposals as saying that the measures were "unnecessary and misguided" and seemed "deliberately designed to discriminate against part-time work". British officials were also quoted as saying that the Commission's argument, that a qualified majority vote would be appropriate in the Council as differences in benefit levels etc. distorted competition between member states, was "spurious". Government spokesmen are also identified as having said the measures would increase unemployment and disrupt the social security system.

Subsequently the Confederation of British Industry (reported in the *Financial Times* for 17 September, 1990) published a response saying that "added costs would force employers to reduce the number of part-time and temporary contracts". The Engineering Employers Federation has replied on similar lines ("damaging and unnecessary" etc.).

Such responses seem to be caught in a serious logical dilemma. *If* the treatment of part-time and temporary workers in Britain *has* been characterised by major discrimination in pay and conditions, together with employer manipulation of hours and lengths of contract to avoid social security obligations, then it cannot be said that such patterns of behaviour do not distort competition in the common market. This is the more evident since the *scale* of part-time employment, etc., is large in the UK and growing. If it is to be argued that there is *little* implication in all this for direct and indirect labour costs, then it must be inappropriate to suggest — as the CBI does — that Directives on part-time workers and on working time could jeopardise the hours and earnings of large numbers of people. We do not believe that there *is* such a risk arising from the Directives, but our point here is that the critics can hardly throw *both* sets of arguments into the debate at the same time.

The evidence that has been summarised in this chapter, drawing entirely on recent official statistics for the UK and officially sponsored labour market surveys and analysis, does, we think, demonstrate the necessity — indeed urgency — of implementing the main proposals of the draft Directives on part-time and temporary work. It is necessary both in terms of the economics of the single market and the social principles on which the Community needs to stand.

Competition based on labour market practices of discrimination, and the manipulation (essentially, avoidance) of various kinds of social security provision to reduce labour costs, is not compatible with the notion of a "level playing field" for business. It is as offensive as would be large-scale discrimination on grounds of sex or race. Indeed, it *is* so offensive because discrimination directed at part-time workers is *overwhelmingly* discrimination directed at *women* workers; while such discrimination continues it directly and indirectly curtails the objectives of equal pay for equal value, and equal opportunity. To tolerate the continuation of such conditions of discrimination and denial of pro rata rights is to retreat from *basic* social rights for people in the Community, to rights for *some*; it is to retreat *further* from harmonisation and cohesion in the Community.

In taking the attitude it has, the UK Government is directly contradicting its *declared* concerns. *Individual* opportunity and prosperity is denied. It denies, for part-time workers etc., its own statement that "If Europe is to prosper in the 1990s investment in training for skills and jobs is vital". It denies its statements on equal opportunities for men and women (e.g. "Britain is firmly committed to equality of opportunity". Are we to add, "but not for 4½ million part-time women workers?"). Or is it taking its stand on semantics and arguing that *both* 900,000 male part-timers in the UK *and* 4½ million female part-timers are *equally unequal, equally subject to discrimination* in pay, conditions, social security (partly denied them), and training (in practice almost wholly denied them).*

The UK Government is also denying its own analysis. This emphasises that the very forms of work contract for which the draft Directive is designed to secure fair standards, are "dynamic" and growing:

> "Throughout Europe women are expected to move into the labour market in increasing numbers . . . Employers are already having . . . to look harder at part-time and flexible forms of working . . . Employers will need to . . . look at

*Quotations in this paragraph are taken from the Department of Employment fact-pack, *People, Jobs, and Progress*, 1989.

the needs of workers, and *meet* those needs, to attract the workers their businesses require . . . In the UK . . . women will account for over 90 per cent of . . . projected labour force growth". (*Op.cit.*, Fact sheet 2.)

And is it really to be understood that all this should develop on the basis of permitted discrimination and denial of social rights for these increasing numbers of women workers and part-time jobs? And does it really make sense to suggest that such continued discrimination (with its direct and indirect cost implications) could be of minimal competitive impact?

UK employer arguments on this subject lack integrity as well as rationality. The CBI knows that the rapidly growing employment problems, and loss of competitiveness, of the UK economy are the fruits of combined and connected policies of long-sustained exceptionally high interest rates and an unduly high exchange rate. Alongside such factors the cost implications of the Commission's proposals on part-time and temporary work are modest indeed and would develop over a period of time. (To be realistic, if the Community proposals are adopted they will tend to come into operation in the next business cycle upswing, circa 1992-1993.)

We have, of course, had similar arguments before, in earlier resistance to equal pay for equal work, and then equal pay for equal value. As the UK government and employers both know (see the quotation above) the main labour reserve that European economic expansion has to tap is that of women workers; the trend will be — as it has been for two decades in Britain — to increase female employment whether women workers are discriminated against or whether they are not. It is, in the long run, more rational to offer pay and working conditions that do not discriminate and exploit. (*Is* the best recruitment slogan, Come and work for us, we will discriminate against you and hinder your development and opportunities?)

In the UK we have even had the allegedly rational and European newspaper *The Financial Times* arguing editorially in response to the Commission's proposals:

"The interests of part-timers and temporary workers will also hardly be served by an enforced harmonisation of their conditions with full-timers throughout the EC. Employers would then substitute full-time for part-time employment, and make such workers truly 'atypical' once more".

This is, of course, rather remarkably arguing that workers have an "interest" in being discriminated against. Even if there were *some* merit in the argument that follows about 'substitution', the real position would be one in which workers who are being discriminated against *all* have an interest in the removal of such restraints on pay, conditions and opportunities but there may be *some* element of job risk. The argument must surely be *least* applicable to temporary workers who are at risk anyway.

What the *FT* comments ignore is the clearcut reality that there are a number of reasons why particular employers will want to employ part-time workers rather than full-time. One obvious factor will be labour supply conditions in local labour markets; firms may find it difficult to recruit and retain full-time workers without raising pay/conditions. In these often repeated conditions, firms will actively seek part-time workers (a good example is provided by the National Health Service in recruiting nursing staff). But there are often important gains from using part-timers which would still operate even if all their conditions were improved to fully 'pro rata' levels. For instance retail traders need to match variations in activity levels (especially with extended opening hours) and levels of staffing; the required flexibility and efficiency involves extensive use of part-time labour to match high levels of activity. This need for flexibility extends not only around the week but in a wide range of industries and services to seasonal peaks and troughs. In addition, access to part-time labour leads to important cost savings even if full 'pro rata' pay is involved; the firm is able to use capital equipment — again, desirably, over an extended range of hours — *without* attracting additional wage costs from paying full-time labour premium rates (overtime, unsocial hours payments).

The notion that there would be an extensive return to full-time employment is consequently a myth. In a similar way critics at one time argued that "equal pay" would be harmful to female employment, but female employment continues its disproportionate increase — as compared with male employment — under conditions of equal pay for equal value. What *will* change is that if the Commission's proposals are put into practice, employers will make rational choices as to the employment of either (or both) full-time or part-time employees, based on productivity, work load, utilisation of plant and equipment, and so on, but *not* based on discriminatory treatment of particular categories. They will be less able to treat their workers in an inequitable way. Technically, using the vocabulary of the economist, an important element of discriminatory monopsonistic exploitation will have been removed.

More positively, once the elements of discriminatory treatment and associated manipulation of working time are removed, we can expect the development of more *rational flexibility* in the handling of patterns or working time. With the extension of the norms attaching to what we now call "full-time" work to virtually all other categories of workers, the *rigidity* of conventional "full-time" work may be reduced. In the future the rational employer may be prepared to develop, in a planned and agreed way, ranges of average weekly working time (all involving equal status and pro rata pay equality) rather than a rigidly determined level of "normal" hours. (We know already that for many "full-time" women workers the hours in the "normal" week are uncomfortably high.) Bargaining about working time can more readily provide for options and flexibility once the stigma of discrimination is removed from work that is less than "full-time".

**Conclusion**
Our analysis of the situation regarding part-time and temporary work confirms the approach and objectives of the Commission in putting forward its proposals for 'pro rata' treatment. The arguments advanced in opposition to this are at the heart mutually contradictory. The alleged harmful implications for employment would appear to have no validity; they do not appear to take account of the real

situation in labour markets or the forward projections as to the characteristics of additional labour supply. They appear to be resorting to rhetorical claims in defence of an element of profitability and competitive advantage that has been built on an inequitable discrimination as to pay and conditions that properly deserves the title of exploitation.

Indeed, the measures proposed should be seen as a touchstone as to the Community's moral integrity in constructing the single market. These areas of employment contract under discussion represent a major segment of the European labour market in which discrimination and lack of opportunity for development is explicit and widespread. Competitive advantage should not be built on such foundations. A "single market" cannot be based on such double standards. A wider public than the workers directly involved should recognise that denial of social rights in this area would profoundly damage the prospects for a Europe that respects its own people.

PART THREE

# THE COMMUNITY'S
# SOCIAL DIMENSION:
# CRITICAL PERSPECTIVES

CHAPTER 6

# Underlying Principles:
# Is the Community's
# Approach Adequate?

*"Le mieux est l'ennemi du bien".*
(Voltaire)

Perhaps it is best to start with an assertion, and one in the spirit of Voltaire's quotation. The Commission's social policies, so far, are directly concerned with a *limited* process of becoming, that of the construction of the single market. This is an understandable phase, and a necessary short to medium-term objective. But they are not — yet — about a wider process of becoming, they do not seek out innovatory models, best practice; there is, perhaps, at least some element of risk that they may inhibit the more socially advanced patterns of behaviour.

The Social Charter will need to mobilize popular sympathy and active support, to capture the adhesion of major institutions and governments, to work hard on a mass of enabling detail, in order to come through across its whole range of concerns and in good time. And yet it is a modest document, and much of the time is concerned to construct *minima*. It is of the nature of its current function that it should. It is not a matter of levelling up to the *best* practice, but of recognising the risks (in a cost and profit orientated world) of European good or "best" practice being undermined (potentially, displaced) if no minima are established, or if the minima are set too low, or are not adequately observed in practice. Operating credible legislation that can be enforced is a critical aspect of what is being attempted. Managing to assert minimum European social rights in practice is an important dimension of freedom; even to assert such *minimum* rights, there are many employers who will have to be (as Rousseau put it) "forced to be free".

Our first critical point of departure should therefore be to ask moderately whether the Commission's proposals go far enough in managing this "minimum" process. There are actually some major sins of omission:

(i) The Commission is far too low key in its approach to minimum wages. Over generations, as ILO practice has shown, persistent attention to legislation on minimum wages and on agencies to manage and monitor the processes involved has been an important positive influence in the world's labour markets. Of course, it is too early to think of a European minimum wage as such, but it is all too late to be tackling the question of the standards, the criteria, that national governments should be using, and to put a floor to pay inequality that has some impact in practice. UK experience in the last decade has been profoundly reactionary; Wages Councils with regulatory mechanisms and statutory minima that have evolved and improved over most of this century have been severely emasculated, the Wages Inspectorate has been deliberately reduced in size to limit effective enforcement, in all major sectors and occupational groups pay inequality has widened dramatically.* The Commission should not "pass by on the other side".

(ii) The Commission seems substantially, in its enunciation of social rights, to have neglected the consumer interest — both individual and collective. Are, for example, information and consultation rights *only* to be of relevance to employed workers? Unfortunately its own practice in this respect is conspicuously inadequate. (Consideration of the consumer interest is discussed more fully later in this chapter.)

(iii) Apart from the question of social responsibilities in the private sector of the economy, there are important questions to address in the conduct of public services and local and national government. One would have hoped that the Community would have been discussing the *lead* that public sectors within the Community could give in establishing patterns of good practice. This seems noticeably lacking. Why

*On pay inequality see *Pay in the 1980s*, Trade Union Research Unit, Ruskin College, August 1990 (25 pages).

should participation etc. of the labour force as of right be restricted to certain kinds of large enterprise; since the Action Programme says it wants to "generalise" such practice, why should it not raise the question of public services and industries in that context? The Commission is also disturbingly weak in its approach to public contracts; the Action Programme says it "*could* formulate a proposal aiming at the introduction of a 'social clause' into public contracts". This is both tentative (its text ought to say "will" not "could") and remarkably lacking in definition or any sense of urgency. "Fair wage" clauses may have a long history, but in the UK they have been removed — and should urgently be restored. Their absence clearly distorts competition in the market. If the UK government wishes to engage in "social dumping" in the handling of public contracts — as evidently it does — that lack of principle should be challenged now and explicitly, not be left to drag on. The UK Government should be forced either to abandon its practices or be seen publicly (in the run-up to a general election) to be challenged on them by the Commission and seen in public to be defending the indefensible.

(iv) When Jacques Delors spoke to the TUC in 1988 he referred to "three proposals . . . designed to show clearly the social dimension of the European construction". The third of these was: "The extension to all workers of the right to life-long education". This was clearly meant to go beyond the accustomed emphasis on vocational education. Why has the line gone dead? Education, as against vocational training, features not at all in the Social Charter (or the subsequent Action Programme). It would be refreshing to have sight of a genuine Commission initiative on this front, which is crucial to a participatory democracy. Delors appeared to be offering a three-legged stool for the "social dimension" to rest on; he must know that two-legged stools are less adequate.

But the argument does need to travel beyond the somewhat constrained scope of the present social principles and proposals.

This is partly a conceptual matter. In a way it is helpful to have the current Community approach of distinguishing between "social aspects" and "economic aspects" of the construction of the single market, and demanding equal attention to both. But that simple first formulation must be *transcended* both in principle and in practice. The European Community throughout its history has been too ready to treat "economic" as identical with "commercial". If we are to measure truly so far as economic benefits and costs are concerned, we need to measure both commercial costs *and* social costs (e.g. pollution costs, congestion costs, etc.), and we need to measure both commercial benefits *and* social benefits. Thus, a commercial enterprise with strong education and training programmes secures some commercial benefits for itself but also confers a wider benefit over time in enhancing the skill endowment and competence of its workers, in ways which may bring no direct benefit to its own revenue account. A *true* economic analysis and accountancy is a socially responsible one (though as economists we may quarrel about the measurement process); a narrow commercial accountancy is measuring parts, not the whole. Competition conducted on the basis of the *latter* may damage and destroy; its labour practices, prices, and products may be distorted and destructive compared with those that are based on a wider accountancy. In other words, for the *economic* benefits of the single market — in a comprehensive sense — to come through, we need firms to be responding to the signalling of all the commercial and social costs and benefits that relate to their activities.

In addition, we need more attention to major *connections* between social and economic policy, instead of their dis-connection under separate headings. *Some* initiatives and practice of this kind are coming through, others are not. Thus, in a way the Commission treats the organisation and expenditure of "structural funds" as outside the Social Charter. Yet the rights and needs of the *unemployed* are within the Charter, but inadequately — very inadequately — dealt with; since so little is being offered them, at least the Charter could *commit* the Community to continuing major expenditure on "structural funds" as part of the basic rights and opportunities being offered the unemployed.

Let us take an example where the connection should be made, but is not. The Social Charter has eloquent sections on freedom of movement but is silent on *housing*. What the European labour market needs (and particularly those citizens disadvantaged within it) is a far bolder approach to "social housing" development across the Community. With a recession developing (1990-1991) it is a good moment to point out that to "construct" a more positive single market by 1992 we could do with a large and sustained burst of social housing expenditure (not least in the UK where the private housing market has collapsed, a victim to its own excesses). Any moderate Keynesian can see the rationality of the Commission and Council of the Community establishing a major programme, based on direct borrowing by the Community itself, of social housing provision — and linked in to the development thrust of the "structural funds" in part, but to the needs of young low-income workers, etc., besides. Not only would this identify in *practice* the growing reality of the social rights (mobility) there on paper, it would represent *no* economic burden to any member state, would reduce structural unemployment, and would more than pay for itself in the medium term so far as the Community was concerned (income from rents, etc.). Mr Delors spoke about the need for people to be "architects" of the single market; in this field of housing he ought to take what he said literally. The point being made here is that *such* an approach would *inter-connect* social concerns and economic concerns; it would enhance the flexibility and efficiency of the forthcoming single market in economic terms while underpinning social rights and opportunities, particularly for currently disadvantaged groups. It is hardly necessary to add that adult education and training is yet another field where the *connection* of social and economic principles and needs has yet to be identified in Community practice.

What else should characterise the underlying principles of the Community in its approach to the social dimension? One thing is glaringly obvious. It should make up for lost time in its approach to *consumers* and to the *communities* they live in. If it has learnt aright what was argued above about the *inclusion* of social costs and benefits into its economic calculus, a fresh approach should come easier.

Let us illustrate what is involved by two simple examples. The Commission prides itself on its breakthrough in taking a commanding initiative in the field of health and safety at the workplace; rightly so. But why adopt an obsolescent approach? The worker but also the consumer is concerned with *product safety*. The collective of consumers in the shape of local communities is deeply and directly concerned with the safety of processes, and of emissions (cf. chemical and nuclear contamination). In that case, there should be more recognition of this in Directives, for example, a fresh look at arrangements for information and consultation. The proposed Directive relating to the disabled, "to ensure that workers with motor disabilities can move in complete safety within the Community, particularly in the working environment" offers an outstanding opportunity — from the beginning of the Community's own consultation process — to embrace a wider community of social partners including the organisations of the disabled themselves.

The second example relates to vocational training. Consumers and their organisations have a powerful and direct interest in the quality and comprehensiveness of vocational training. It is in their interest, especially when purchasing complex products or services, to have informed and suitably skilled staff with an ability to communicate effectively. On the other hand, they would not wish to be at the receiving end of the kind of "training" programme which has equipped staff to use techniques of pressurised selling. It would be a most important development if consumer concerns and principles of consumer protection were a feature of many vocational training programmes, and if consumer interests were involved in the development and design of such training. This applies not only in the commercial field but in social services where consumer rights and needs should be recognised in principle and practice (e.g. in health and education services).

Of course, as an organised movement, consumer interests are far less effectively organised than, for instance, trade unions, and have fewer resources (in finance and available specialised staff). But this should mean that the Commission should be positive in its support and encouragement of such movements and of their role in Community consultative processes, *without* for its part attempting to dominate or "capture" consumerism. There can hardly be said to be cost constraints in this; if the Community had encouraged and developed an effective and specialised advocacy of consumer interests it is hardly conceivable that we should have seen such vast resources devoted to the Common Agricultural Policy on the scale and in the forms in which they were. Effective consumerism can be a major ingredient in accountability and better allocation of resources.*

One objection to certain kinds of commercially orientated consumerism is that it is concerned with the interests of the "haves" rather than the "have nots". It is assumed here that the Commission and the Community would instead be particularly supportive of the kind of consumerism that seeks to represent the needs and views of the "disadvantaged and inarticulate" consumer; this would include the kinds of organisations which in the UK we call the "poverty lobby". Indeed, how else could the Commission develop in practice initiatives on sections of the Social Charter relating to "minimum income" and "social protection" for the elderly, and for other disadvantaged groups, except in consultation with the active consumerism of the disadvantaged?

Finally, another adjunct to the Commission's present programme of social initiatives is called for. It is, simply, an active attempt to identify "best practice" and progressive new models of activity and organisation across the employment and social field within the member states. What this approach would invite would be an admixture of support and assistance where relevant, independent monitoring and evaluation, and a wide spread of publicity and information to encourage others in social initiatives and more advanced industrial relations practice. We are not here talking about 'harmonisation', but rather welcoming the diversity of creativity and integrity of purpose. That should be as much a part of the *identity* of the Community as the concern (necessary concern) with minima. But the latter is about the

---

*The doubting reader is referred on this subject to the National Consumer Council's *Consumers and the Common Agricultural Policy*, published by Her Majesty's Stationery Office, 170 pages of text and over 100 pages of Appendices. Agriculture in the EC is in business terms a very uneven playing field indeed, on occasion indeed mountainous — and often shrouded in mist (or mystification).

*last* agenda of social practice and purpose, the former is about the *next* agenda.

A current and extraordinarily interesting case of innovatory action is the programme agreed between Ford UK and its trade unions under the title of the "Employee Development and Assistance Programme", which extends to *all* Ford workers financial and organisational support in self-selected programmes of *educational* activity, jointly managed and helped forward by plant level committees. This is *not* another exercise in vocational training (that is handled as a quite separate matter), it is egalitarian and shared, and has already led to dramatically high take-up.* It is interesting that this shift to a 'high trust' industrial relations practice should come out of a relatively sophisticated but adversarial system of company-wide collective bargaining. It *could*, used as a model, be a transforming influence in workers' education.

A more socially progressive Europe will be helped forward by a European Commission and Council that reaches out to stimulate, support, and publicize advanced and advancing practice that can be re-worked and improved upon in other initiatives throughout the Community. In a way, the sooner such new models and better practice take off the more quickly will the Social Charter of 1989 become out-dated and require re-drafting to fit a felt need for new norms of social rights.

---

*See Trade Union Research Unit: EDAP Questionnaire Survey 1989, Final Report for Hourly Paid and Salaried Employees (published April 1990).

# CHAPTER 7

# Next Steps for the Trade Unions in Europe

UK trade unions have begun to travel towards some of the Continental norms of trade union rights and responsibilities. Understandably, this shift was heavily influenced by the recognition that on a range of policy matters the European Commission (particularly as embodied in its President) represented friendly allies, in sharp contrast to the expressed hostility of the UK Government. The Commission's approach was built round a more than purely formal recognition of the trade unions in Europe as representing a key "social partner" with whom consultation and "dialogue" took place in a generally consensual style, and to whom collective bargaining represented not only a socially relevant way of determining pay and conditions, but also a valid contribution to a wider industrial democracy. Suddenly, the UK trade unions had a sense not of *their* comparative isolation and defensive retreat, but of their place in a powerful and advancing coalition of forces in Europe; by contrast, they could begin to recognise the comparative isolation of the UK Government and *its* awkwardly conducted defensive retreat. For the Government could not secure a "single market" without previously accepting important constitutional changes — in the direction of federal government of the socio-economic system — that could override a UK veto.

For a time this shift may seem less than the radical and developing process it will prove to be, for a variety of reasons. The first is that it feels very much as if the TUC itself is enjoying the experience of participating again in corporatist influence and policy making at the top, but now within the European institutions rather than at home. We can hardly even say that the process is a "top down" one, since it seems to stay largely at the top. In two senses; one is that a good deal of the 'action' is *cerebral*, advancing ideas and objectives in committee proceedings, rather than concerned with re-thinking *into* operational strategies the developing possibilities for trade union functions in the place of work and the enterprise. The other is that the processes and procedures are unduly confined to a network of liaison and representation at a level of formal exchange that meshes in with the elaborated bureaucracy and emasculated parliamentary democracy of the European Community, rather than anything else.

The second reason that the shift towards a European dimension and framework of industrial relations practice seems slow to emerge within British trade unionism is that many trade unions, especially at the moment those in the public sector, are having to grapple with the issues and consequences involved in a swift and pervasive shift to decentralised bargaining in place of the old stable centralised processes. This sets up new pressures on resources and the quality of services provided to memberships facing new patterns of employer organisation and behaviour. In the commercial sector of the economy the onset of a recession, clumsily produced by Government mismanagement of the previous boom and its aftermath, is rapidly producing its own set of difficulties and displacement for workers and 'firefighting' for the unions.

In these circumstances, a sense of direction and of strategy seems slow to emerge. We do not even have — though it is now important to develop it — any comprehensive survey as to what individual trade unions, or industrial groupings of trade unions are actually doing, on the ground, in shaping new institutional responses with their counterparts in Europe, and in developing new agendas, campaigns, and patterns of industrial action. But, for instance, the interplay between the earlier industrial action of the German metalworkers on reduction of the working week, and the powerfully developed industrial action of the British engineering unions in 1989-90 (in a different and more decentralised bargaining context) for the same objectives is sign enough of new movement, determination and purpose.

As a prelude to the next stage of wider European orientated development, it may be worth attempting to identify what some key areas of initiative should be, and what fresh problems — as well as opportunities — they will throw up for organised labour.

To start with, the argument of earlier sections of this book should be recalled. The analysis pointed to a fairly protracted — possibly, uncomfortably delayed — process of putting in place in broadly *legislative* terms a framework of minimum provisions concerning employment and other social rights, both individual and collective. That process is not only developing with time-lags, it is influenced by various employer and governmental pressures, and parts of it may emerge in a watered-down form. For all the talk of "harmonisation", there may be less "levelling up" than there should be. We should beware of having served up to us merely a codification of *yesterday's* 'good' industrial relations or social policy practice. So for the trade unions, the perspective should not be to wait for a new Europeanised version of the old 'state socialism' to deliver in decrees the promised land.

This is a situation that calls for considered and sustained trade union pressure. Given its history, the British trade union movement would not find it unusual to be presented with the need to co-ordinate two kinds of pressure, industrial and political. Let us take, for instance, the issue of "pro rata" treatment of part-time workers, dealt with in detail in an earlier chapter. In many cases trade unions have already won "pro rata" treatment through their organisational and bargaining work, at least on pay. But that is far from universal and not in all cases followed through into equality in conditions — and least of all into access to training. Nor, where temporary workers are accepted as part of the system, are they fully protected or guaranteed opportunity to move to permanent status. But "best practice" in bargaining achievement can be used, together with the argument that legally imposed norms will be on their way, to increase organisational and bargaining pressure for improvement in the treatment and opportunities of such workers *now*. Alongside that, wider publicity and campaigning directed at part-time workers (but also at full-time workers, especially women workers, in the name of fairness and equal rights) should build moral support for action and political opposition to UK Government defence of discrimination. After all, when the European Community's Directive goes through it will need to be translated into UK legislation, and that in its turn can be stronger than it might otherwise have been if there is sufficient popular understanding of what principles are at stake and what reform could mean in practice.

In other words, across many of the subject areas covered by the Social Charter the British (and other European) trade unions should be developing in the domain of collective bargaining their own proposals for a "social dimension" in preparation for the single market, in terms both of substantive agreements and new procedural agreements too. This should develop in advance of the wave of legislation at national levels that the European Council's Directives will induce, but in anticipation of it. There are very good reasons of self-interest why many employers will prefer to retain trust in their internal labour market and an edge in recruitment in their external labour markets by working out in their own practice what will later be required of them in some form by legislation. Such an approach in collective bargaining terms would help underpin and give a realistic setting for the wider trade union campaigning for the full (undiluted) and early realisation of the Community-wide social Action Programme.

An approach on these lines does not have to be piecemeal, nor must it be empty rhetoric. What would be particularly beneficial would be cross-frontier co-operation by trade unions so that within specific transnational European enterprises (or wider multinationals) "social dimension" collective bargaining demands are put forward in a co-ordinated way. That does not mean *identical* demands, but rather the relevant demands that would *level up* to better or best practice across the whole enterprise; thus, the existing "best" practice in country A could be used as the basis for demands by the trade unions in countries B and C. Rather than a scatter-gun approach, what is called for is a more strategic selection of objectives and of sectors and companies, and a determination to make a significant advance (*pour encourager les autres*) in those selected. In another sense, an ounce of carefully chosen new practice is worth a ton of paper proposals. What the previous paragraph is pointing to is the supreme importance of getting off the ground and into working order even a small set of fully developed bargained agreements and participatory arrangements right across some major Euro-firms. Of course, this poses a challenge — of imagination, organisation, and re-examination of vested interest — to the trade unions that would need to be concerned. But the *learning* process cannot come too soon. This is about *more* than the traditional domain of trade union recognition, plant level workers' representation, bargained pay, conditions, and controls on working time; though they are all *part* of what is involved. It is about the subject areas that used to carry the label of industrial democracy (or even workers' control). It is about testing in practice what a fully participative system in a major transnational enterprise will involve under conditions of effective trade unionism.

One can perceive what some of the crucial issues of principle and practice will be:
—Quite how do the trade unions relate to the employee-based representational systems needed within each plant *and* at the other levels through to 'top' decision-making? The trade unions will have to accept not simply a *formal* separation of at least some aspects of workers' representation within the enterprise from the direct control of trade unions. (Remember that legislative rights of participation will relate to *all* employees.) The trade unions will need to offer support of many kinds (one thinks of the large-scale training and development commitment for their members playing key roles in co-determination that the German trade unions had to develop), not least in offering inter-firm experience,* but for a variety of reasons they should not be trying to take "institutional capture" to the point where they seek the incorporation of an organised democracy that should develop a degree of identity of its

---

*The European trade union movements most involved with such systems used to refer to the problem of "enterprise narrowness" that emerged.

own. There is — certainly in British experience — a danger that otherwise the tensions that can arise between the interests and attitudes of different unions can slow down and complicate an enterprise-based participatory system that needs to develop coherence and a strategic sense.

—There are problems, from the trade union side, of resource constraints. These will need to be tackled from two directions. Firstly, what *will* prove to be incompatible is the extension of workers' and trade unions' functions and an attempt to deliver trade unionism *cheaply*. British trade union membership dues have quite simply to be increased considerably; they have in a number of areas of competitive overlap been held down unduly. Defensive trade union mergers have been more about an effort (often frustrated) to build in economies of larger scale in face of financial crises than about a strategic re-grouping to face new needs — and more powerful and subtle employers. Secondly, the new functions for workers and their representatives *within* the enterprise need to be provided for by agreements on *facilities* that will enable a genuine process of company-wide information, consultation, and participation to operate effectively and intelligently. There has to be a battle for the enterprise to concede the *means* as well as being forced by Euro-legislation to concede the *ends*.

—It sounds a natural development of the system to say that workers and their representatives will have tangible rights to participate in the decisions that shape company *development*. In fact it is a very testing area that carries its full weight of social responsibilities. Development is a polite word for what Schumpeter two generations ago rightly called "creative destruction" (sometimes the destruction is more obvious than the creativity), as changing technology and competition between giant firms alters the industrial landscape. Certainly, it is quite as much about displacement as it is about growth; and it is consequently about where (locationally) the destruction takes place and where the creation. Understandably this represents scope for considerable tension between employees (and their trade unions) in different countries; that has to be faced and if possible transcended. All this will be taking place under the shadow of speculative capital markets and predatory processes of take-over and merger (an enterprise these days is not a tidy, stable, organisation but often an all-too-rapidly re-shuffled portfolio of assets being manipulated — they call it "management" — for all too short-run reasons). What this should tell us is that the trade unions should recognise that they need *alongside* the new enterprise industrial relations systems the establishment of effective instruments of social control (not least in scrutiny of take-over proposals, and in physical and environmental controls) together with evolving European "structural funds".

—In another sense than reaching out to necessary social controls over large enterprise, the trade unions will need to avoid the slogan of "ourselves alone". They need to be working in alliance with local — and regional — communities. This, of course, particularly concerns the impact of the firm (in its processes *and* its products) on the environment. This is a necessary dimension of social responsibility that should be built into the thinking of the trade unions from the start of their deliberations about the Euro-wide enterprise. The scale of this problem in Eastern Europe (and therefore now within part of Germany) is a reminder of how important it is that new European models of industrial democracy should bring the communities of Europe into their strategic thinking. But it is not only about pollution, it is, among other things, about congestion costs and the need to rescue public transport systems, it is about *facilities* accessible to workers in their local communities to enable organisation and international exchange to operate with less constraint.

—One of the "facilities" must assume special importance in the new context. Euro-industrial democracy must make full use of the new and rapidly evolving information technology, and it must find effective ways of handling multi-lingual exchange between workers while so doing. (Of course, that should mean masses of in-plant languages classes and facilities — as has emerged even in the first year of the new Ford UK employee development programme mentioned in an earlier chapter.) The "old" trade union democracy was built round 19th Century developments; the telephone, the railway, conference centres, mechanical office equipment, simple filing systems. It can't cope with the new needs, its costs are too high and its flexibility too limited. The trade unions of Europe therefore have to design and then operate new systems and linkages that can rapidly be implemented by trade unions of several countries acting in association. (Ideally, the telecommunications trade unions of Europe should use their special skills and understanding to pioneer what is called for in 21st century trade union organisational terms.) But in addition, a *crucial* test of the *reality* of industrial democracy is how far the employees and their representatives within each major transnational firm can utilise the elaborated communication technology of their own firm (including taking from it the information they need about the enterprise); indeed, it is a matter of how far the firm in further development of its information technology (including video and computer conferencing, for instance) will modify or extend its systems to encompass their needs.

To raise such questions is only to climb the next set of foothills facing the organised labour forces of Europe. There are more profound questions of structure and purpose yet to come, but they are beyond the scope of this chapter. But we can all understand that the old *nationally* based structures of trade unionism have to move much further towards federation and joint working, both as movements inside those old frontiers and as trade unions operating on a continental and international scale. In this there may appear to be much to learn from capital's capacity to operate internationally. But that model won't suffice; it does not start off from the principle of democracy, and accountability to its members, as any trade union must. It does not start off with *respect* for the variety of cultures that any wider trade union movement must reflect. Perhaps we can put the agenda *after* next as ensuring that the capacity of the trade unions of Europe to develop federated organisation and activity across frontiers and on a fully democratic basis moves *at least as fast* as the developing federalism of what Toynbee would have called the European superstate.

*That* superstate in its evolution so far has already exhibited what we have learned to call a "democratic deficit". The next agenda for the Community *beyond* the Social Charter will have to be the correction of that democratic deficit. But the European trade unions must ensure that they do not fall into the same trap as they move into a Europe without frontiers.

# APPENDIX

# 1992:
# A Check-list on the Social Dimension

*Hugh McMahon* MEP

The Social Charter was signed in December 1989 by eleven of the twelve Member States of the European Community — only the United Kingdom did not sign.

The Charter, drafted at the suggestion of the Council of Ministers for Social Affairs, and consolidated by Jacques Delors, President of the European Commission, did not find complete favour with MEPs, who felt that it was no more than a solemn declaration without any force of law behind it. However, the Charter, even in its rather weak form, was at least a move in the right direction towards social protection in the Internal Market.

A further step towards improving working conditions was taken in November 1989, when the Commission produced the Action Programme on the Social Charter: a series of specific measures in the social field, which would come under Community law. Too mild, still, from the European Parliament's point of view, the Action Programme gave rise to an own initiative Report by the Parliament's Social Affairs Committee, the Van Velsen Report, which presented Parliament's own position on the whole social area.

The following check-list compares the positions of the Social Charter itself, that of the Action Programme, and that of the European Parliament. An update of the legislative situation is given where possible, although at the moment, relatively few pieces of relevant legislation have been introduced by the Commission. The Parliament is currently pressing for more, and better, legislation to be brought forward.

## Freedom of Movement

*Social Charter*
The right to freedom of movement shall enable any worker to engage in any occupation or profession in the Community, in accordance with the principles of equal treatment as regards access to employment, working conditions, and social protection in the host country.

*Action Programme*
The Commission proposes to revise a Regulation on the right of workers to remain on the territory of a Member State after having been employed there; proposes to apply social security schemes to employed and self-employed persons and their families moving within the Community; proposes to introduce a labour clause into public contracts applying in other countries; and will publish a Communication on workers in frontier regions of the EC.

*European Parliament*
The European Parliament considers it necessary to take the above measures further, by recognising the right to unemployment benefits for workers who go to settle in a country other than that where they had their last employment; it wishes to fix social payments in such a way as to avoid double taxing of boundary workers; it advocates a Directive which grants to nationals of third countries, having legally stayed for five years in the Community, the same rights of freedom of movement and residence as Member States' citizens.

## Employment, Remuneration and the Labour Market

*Social Charter*
All employment should be fairly remunerated. To this end, all workers shall be assured of an equitable wage; workers subject to atypical terms of employment shall benefit from an equitable reference wage; wages may be withheld only in accordance with national law, but the individual must still have the means of subsistence for himself/herself and family.

*Action Programme*
The Commission suggest Action Programmes on employment creation for specific target groups; it proposes to monitor and re-evaluate the European Social Fund; it will ask only for an Opinion on the introduction of an equitable wage by the Member States; and has already published proposals for Directives on contracts and employment relationships other than full-time open ended contracts (The Atypical Work Directive).

*European Parliament*
The European Parliament has already drafted its alternative to the Commission's Draft Directive on Atypical Work, requesting that the legal base of the legislation be changed to require only majority voting, rather than the unanimity needed at present; the Parliament also demands a Draft Directive which establishes a minimum salary on the basis of Article 118a (majority voting).

The Socialists on the Social Affairs Committee are already working on this; they ask for a Commission Programme of Action aimed at achieving full employment; equality between Community and extra-Community citizens is expected; the Parliament suggests the creation of a European Council on Employment made up of trade unions and employers, entrusted with the signing of collective agreements.

## Improvement of Living and Working Conditions

*Social Charter*
The process must result from an approximation of conditions, as regards, in particular, the duration and organisation of working time and forms of employment; the procedure must cover such aspects of employment as collective redundancies and bankruptcies; every worker must have a weekly rest period and annual paid leave and a contract of employment.

*Action Programme*
The Commission has published a Directive for the adaptation of working time on which the Social Affairs Committee is currently drafting a Report; it has also proposed a Directive

on the introduction of a form to serve as proof of an employment contract or relationship.

*European Parliament*
The European Parliament has just published a Report on the Commission's Draft Directive on working time, which demands that day time working should also be included in the Draft Directive which at the moment merely deals with work and overtime carried out at night. Parliament asks that a statutory limit be set on the length of the working week. Parliament also asks for concrete measures which guarantee Community citizens housing which preserves the dignity of the individual.

## Social Protection

*Social Charter*
Every worker in the Community shall have a right to adequate social protection and shall, regardless of status, enjoy an adequate level of social security benefits. Persons outside the labour market must receive sufficient resources and social assistance in keeping with their particular situation.

*Action Programme*
The Commission suggest the publication of a mere recommendation on social protection and, again, a recommendation on common criteria to be used in this field.

*European Parliament*
The European Parliament has called for Directives on social aid, old age pensions, grants for single parent families, maternity and paternity leave, "education" leave, and the maintaining of remuneration in the event of illness or incapacity for a certain duration.

## Freedom of Association and Collective Bargaining, Information, Consultation and Participation

*Social Charter*
Employers and workers shall have the right of association in order to constitute professional organisations or trade unions.

Employers' organisations and trade unions shall have the right to negotiate and conclude collective agreements. There shall be the right to resort to collective action, which includes the right to strike, subject to national legislation. Moreover, information and consultation for workers must apply, especially for companies having establishments in two or more Member States of the Community. Such procedures must be implemented, especially in the cases of technological change, restructuring operations, and collective redundancies.

*Action Programme*
The Commission's contribution amounts to the publication of a communication on the role of the social partners in collective bargaining. It also proposed a Community instrument on the procedures for the information, consultation, and participation of the workers of European-scale undertakings, and an instrument on equity sharing and financial participation by workers.

*European Parliament*
The European Parliament calls for a Directive which guarantees trade union freedom, the right to trade union training, information, consultation and worker participation in companies, as well as protection against arbitrary dismissal.

## Vocational Training

*Social Charter*
Every worker of the European Community must be able to have access to vocational training; there must be no discrimination on the grounds of nationality. The competent authorities should set up training systems to improve workers' skills.

*Action Programme*
The Commission proposes a Community instrument on access to vocational training. It wishes to update a previous Council Decision on a common vocational training policy; and it says it will rationalise programmes in this field. Presently the

Commission is examining proposals for a Directive on the comparability of qualifications.

*European Parliament*
The Parliament calls for a Directive on the right to vocational training; the right to take leave; training for all, including the unemployed.

## Equal Treatment for Men and Women

*Social Charter*
Equal treatment must be assured, and equal opportunities must be developed, in particular as regards access to employment, remuneration, working conditions, social protection, education, vocational training, and career development.

*Action Programme*
The Commission suggest a third Community Programme on equal opportunities; a recommendation concerning child care; a recommendation concerning a code of good conduct on the protection of pregnancy and maternity. More importantly, the Commission has just published a Draft Directive on the protection of pregnant women at work, using Article 118a of the Treaty as a legal base, thus requiring only a majority vote at the Council of Ministers.

*European Parliament*
The European Parliament has called for the provision of a legal base to ensure the respect of "equality" Directives. It also demands a Directive fixing quotas for women in institutions, parties, trade unions, and employers' organisations; it recommends a code of conduct for specific groups (pregnant women and mothers) and for male/female relations at work (in particular, to fight sexual harassment). The Women's Committee of the Parliament is currently studying the Commission's proposals for a Directive on pregnant women and mothers at work.

## Health Protection and Safety at the Workplace

*Social Charter*
Every worker must enjoy satisfactory health and safety conditions in his/her working environment. Appropriate measures must be taken in order to achieve further harmonisation of conditions in this area, while maintaining the improvements made.

*Action Programme*
Commission proposals for Directives apply to the following fields: medical assistance aboard vessels (for which the proposed legislation has just been published); temporary or mobile sites (recently published); workers in the drilling industries; the quarrying and opencast mining industries; fishing vessels; industrial diseases; safety signs at the workplace; dangerous industrial agents; physical agents; exposure to asbestos; transport sector; establishment of a health and safety agency.

*European Parliament*
While endorsing all of the above, the European Parliament also calls for a revision of the Directive on the protection against risks linked to exposure to chemical, physical and biological agents; and asks for initiatives in the fight against drug abuse, and tobacco and alcohol abuse at work.

## Protection of Children and Adolescents

*Social Charter*
The minimun employment age must not be lower than the school leaving age, neither of which must be lower than fifteen years of age. The duration of work must be limited, and night work prohibited, under eighteen years. After compulsory education, young people must be entitled to receive initial vocational training of reasonable duration.

*Action Programme*
The Commission has proposed a Directive on the approximation of the laws of the Member States on the protection of young people.

*European Parliament*
The European Parliament calls for a ban on work by young people under sixteen years of age, and for strict conditions regulating the nature and duration of work and the legal minimum wage.

## The Elderly

*Social Charter*
Every worker of the European Community must, at the time of retirement, be able to enjoy resources affording him/her a decent standard of living, and those not entitled to a pension must be otherwise provided for.

*Action Programme*
The Commission proposes a Community initiative for the elderly (a communication and a proposal for a decision).

*European Parliament*
The following guarantees are also necessary: equal treatment for men and women as regards retirement age and pensions; the flexibility of retirement age; and the right to home care if and when necessary.

## The Handicapped

*Social Charter*
All disabled people must be entitled to additional concrete measures aimed at improving their social and professional integration. These measures must concern vocational training, ergonomics, accessibility, mobility, means of transport, and housing.

*Action Programme*
The Commission proposes a Council Decision establishing a third Action Programme for disabled people for 1992-1996. It also proposes a Directive on the introduction of measures aimed at promoting an improvement in the travel conditions of workers with motor disabilities.

*European Parliament*

The European Parliament asks that the Commission writes into the legislative programme for 1992 a draft Directive aimed at improving the mobility of handicapped workers. It also asks that forms of atypical work especially suited to handicapped people (notably, work at home) be afforded the same social protection as those in other forms of work.

## Current Developments

There are several developments in the pipeline at the moment in the social area as far as Europe is concerned. In the European Parliament, the publication of the own-initiative Van Velsen Report marks a step forward, enabling Parliament to state its own views on the social area.

Secondly, the approach taken to the Commission's Draft Directive on Atypical Work by the Salisch Report has made it clear that Parliament is no longer prepared to accept the Commission's decisions on the appropriate legal bases for legislation in this field. It has become clear that if unanimity is needed for social legislation at Council of Ministers level, then no worthwhile social legislation will ever be agreed.

In this context, the President of the European Commission, Jacques Delors, has said that, at the Intergovernmental Conference, the Commission will propose the extension of majority voting to a wider range of social provisions. At the moment, he says, the current provisions are "obsolete, incomplete and ineffective". The Socialists in the European Parliament could not agree more, and will continue to demand that social legislation is brought suitably up to date.

## Glossary

A *Regulation*, once adopted by the Council of Ministers, will be binding in its entirety and applicable as it stands to all Member States. The Regulation will be published in the *Official Journal of the European Communities*, and will immediately become part of the national law in the twelve Member States.

A *Directive*, though binding on Member States as regards the results to be achieved, the form and method of achieving these results is left to the discretion of national authorities.

A *Decision* is similar in some ways to a Regulation, but may apply not to all Community States, but to one or more (or to individuals).

*Recommendations* and *Opinions* have no legal force in Member States: they are, in effect, merely advice to governments.

# European Union: Fortress or Democracy?

## Towards a Democratic Market and a New Economic Order

MICHAEL BARRATT BROWN

1 992 is not only the year when the European Community becomes a single market, with all the economic implications for associated countries as well as for the twelve members. It will also be the crunch year for Eastern Europe's transition to a market economy, and perhaps most important of all the year when bridges will have to be built from Europe to the peoples of the Third World of developing countries, whose hearts and minds were never won for a military settlement of the Gulf crisis. This book is inspired by the fear that preoccupation with purely European questions will lead to neglect of Europe's responsibility for the desperate situation in the Third World countries, which are almost without exception one-time European colonies.

The author, who is an international economist, examines some of the problems involved in preventing the emergence of a fortress mentality in Europe as a response to the catastrophic situation outside. He raises fundamental questions about the failure of economic command systems in the East to deliver the goods, the equal failure of the capitalist world market to meet the needs of more than a small minority of the world's people, and the disastrous results for all from rising debts and falling incomes in the consequent recourse to internecine struggle and military adventure. In doing so, he offers some suggestions for new forms of economic development, new ways of making the market democratic, and new types of trade relations which are both fairer and more environmentally sustainable.

**Michael Barratt Brown** is a director of the Bertrand Russell Peace Foundation. He was the founding Principal of Northern College. Now he is the Chairman of Third World Information Network and Twin Trading Ltd.

ISBN 0 85124 521 8   £7.95   paper
ISBN 0 85124 520 X   £20.00   cloth
Elf Books 2

SPOKESMAN
for European Labour Forum

# Against a Rising Tide
## Racism, Europe and 1992

### MEL READ MEP and ALAN SIMPSON

*A*gainst a Rising Tide considers how racism and xenophobia form increasingly prominent threads in the tapestry of European economies and societies. At one level, the authors argue, little has changed. European industry has always required cheap labour, and has usually drawn it from former colonies and the Third World. And domestic racism has helped keep this labour mainly poor and forever foreign (irrespective of what it says on your passport or birth certificate). But 1992 will bring contradictions of its own. "Freedom of Movement" will not apply equally throughout the Community. It will depend on citizenship status. Clandestine meetings of foreign ministers are tightening immigration rules and procedures, specifically in relation to Third World countries. Business has found a new source of cheap labour in Eastern Europe. And the extreme Right has found new converts to old prejudices in the crevices of faltering European economies.

The authors explore ways in which those with a different vision — that of a "people's" Europe — might work to move beyond the divisions of prejudice, discrimination, exploitation, and intimidation. Pooling their experience of anti-racist work at local, national, and international levels, and taking Nottingham as an example, they offer practical ways in which local authorities and local people can combat racism, setting this work in a European context. Perhaps most significantly, they challenge us to look at racism in a less fragmented way — seeing citizenship rights, economic exploitation, and the threat of physical attack as inter-related aspects of the new European racism.

**Mel Read** is the Labour Member of the European Parliament for Leicester, Nuneaton and North Warwickshire. She is also Chair of the European Parliamentary Labour Party. Formerly, she was Employment Officer at the Racial Equality Council in Nottingham. She is a lifelong trade union activist and former national executive member of MSF.

**Alan Simpson** is Research Officer for the Racial Equality Council in Nottingham. He is author of several works dealing with racial discrimination in housing, economic policy and the inner cities, community development, and policing policy.

ISBN 0 85124 526 9   £6.95   paper
ISBN 0 85124 525 0   £20   cloth
Elf Books 3

SPOKESMAN
for Nottingham Racial Equality Council
and European Labour Forum

# The TGWU
# Congratulates Elf

In the face of grave challenges to jobs and living standards from Europe 1992, the TGWU congratulates Elf for its work in exploring the basis for creating a united and strong European labour movement, committed to establishing a powerful voice for working people across Europe to challenge the power of regrouped multinational employers and unaccountable government.

The task of renewing working class struggle to face the European challenge is urgent.

It should unite manufacturing and service workers, white and blue collar workers, pensioners and students and parents, men, women, and ethnic groups. Above all, it must develop a strategy for building on the new opportunities brought by the end of the Cold War, by maintaining the unity of industrial and political methods for creating massive pressures for real welfare, real collective and individual rights, and peaceful development.

It is a task already started; in the battles for shorter working hours, for equal pay, for peace. But a wider agenda, and a more forceful commitment to building links at workplace and community level, will be necessary to give real force to existing labour movement connections for co-operation and solidarity.

These are tasks to which the TGWU is committed, in pursuit of its basic aims both to protect working people's living standards and make progress on their just demands for a fair, decent, and peaceful world.

Ron Todd
*General Secretary*

Bill Morris
*Deputy General Secretary*

# Pigs' Meat

## Selected Writings of Thomas Spence
## With an introductory essay and notes by
## G.I. Gallop

THOMAS SPENCE, Radical, land-reformer, dismissed
schoolmaster and poverty-stricken book-pedlar, died at the
age of 64 in 1814 "leaving nothing . . . but an injunction to
promote his Plan and the remembrance of his inflexible
integrity". Soon afterwards, the society which tried to
preach his doctrines was banned by Act of Parliament.

In the story of the emergence of British radicalism and
socialism in the late eighteenth and early nineteenth
centuries, the works of Thomas Spence are an
indispensable element. He produced a comprehensive
argument for political and social revolution based on what
he liked to call the "real" rights of man. Decentralisation,
common ownership, participation and mutuality were
central features of his ideas. We may indeed call him
Britain's "first modern socialist".

This representative collection of his surviving writings,
edited with a detailed introduction by G.I. Gallop, at last
restores to the modern Labour movement a rich part of its
partimony, long neglected and underestimated.

### The selection includes:

### The Rights of Man (1793)

### The End of Oppression (1795)

### A Letter from Ralph Hodge to his Cousin Thomas Bull (1795)

### The Meridian Sun of Liberty (1796)

### The Rights of Infants (1797)

### The Restorer of Society to its Natural State (1803)

"Mr Gallop has done us a considerable service in making
available a good and representative selection of Spence's
writings."

A.L. Morton, *Morning Star*

192 pages     ISBN 0 85124 315 0     Socialist Classics No.2

# The Demilitarized Society
## *Disarmament and Conversion*

### SEYMOUR MELMAN

*The Demilitarized Society* diagnoses the economic and allied decay caused by militarism, and formulates a set of proposals — political and economic — for demilitarizing our societies. It argues for building a coalition to challenge the power of the war-making institutions, composed of those occupations and interests which are deprived by the misapplication of resources to armaments. The deterioration of the infrastructure and productivity of society can only be reversed by the proper use of social capital. Adequate housing, health services, education, roads, public transportation, environmental cleanup, urban renovation, care of our children and the aged are all frustrated by the misuse of the capital fund to build weapons that are too terrible to be used and whose use would result in omnicide.

Industrialized nations — East and West — face this dilemma in common with much of the less developed world. Once the superpowers embark on the simultaneous course of disarmament and economic conversion, it will be in their interest and essentially within their power to ensure that the blocs they control and other nations within their spheres of influence do likewise.

The author provides a reliable "road map" to disarmament which would secure the jobs of those presently employed in military production and administration, and even the legal framework necessary for *all* nations to follow.

Seymour Melman is Professor Emeritus of Industrial Engineering at Columbia University. He is recognised worldwide as a leading authority on arms conversion.

Paper £5.50    ISBN 0 85124 506 4
*from Spokesman, Bertrand Russell House,*
*Gamble Street, Nottingham NG7 4ET*

# Elf

SOCIALIST GROUP
EUROPEAN PARLIAMENT

## European Labour Forum

*Socialism through the back door.*

*Come in!*
*Don't bother to knock!*

**Elf** is a journal of politics edited by Ken Coates MEP.

Subscription details are available from:

Bertrand Russell House
Gamble Street
Nottingham
NG7 4ET
England

Telephone (0)602 708318
Fax (0)602 420433